Voices of Lombard Street

A Century of Change in East Baltimore

DEBORAH R. WEINER
ANITA KASSOF
AVI Y. DECTER
editors

Publication of this catalog was made possible with generous support from:

Henry & Ruth Blaustein
Rosenberg Foundation

Lucius N. Littauer Foundation

Institute of Museum and
Library Services

Maryland Historical Trust

Maryland State Arts Council

Betsey & Philip Kahn
Publications Endowment

Louis & Frances B. Booke
Research Endowment

JEWISH MUSEUM OF MARYLAND

15 LLOYD STREET

BALTIMORE, MARYLAND 21202

410/732-6400

www.jewishmuseummd.org

Catalog design by:

EMILY WILSON

PALOLODEEP DESIGN

emily@palolodeep.com

Table of Contents

Acknowledgments

We express our heartfelt gratitude to the funders who have supported this catalog: the Henry and Ruth Blaustein Rosenberg Foundation and the Lucius N. Littauer Foundation. The exhibition was made possible by grants from the Institute of Museum and Library Services and the Maryland Historical Trust. We are also grateful to our exhibition sponsors, the Attman, Boltansky, and Tulkoff families, all of whom can trace their roots to Lombard Street.

In addition, we offer special thanks to the people whose gracious assistance helped make this catalog possible.

Helen Sollins established the oral history collection at the Jewish Museum of Maryland. The interviews she conducted and collected have greatly enhanced our understanding of life in the old neighborhood.

Curatorial assistant Jennifer Vess worked tirelessly to track down and scan a seemingly endless number of photos.

Museum volunteers Ed Schechter and Jerry Wittik provided valuable research support, diligently combing through sources ranging from the U.S. census to the *Baltimore Jewish Times*.

Dedicated staff at numerous repositories displayed admirable patience no matter how many demands we placed on their time. We are especially grateful to Jennifer B. Bodine, aaubreybodine.com; Eric Holcomb, Baltimore City Commission for Historical and Architectural Preservation; Tom Hollowak, Langsdale Library Special Collections, University of Baltimore; Jeff Korman, Maryland Department, Enoch Pratt Free Library; Pat Leader, *Baltimore Sun*; Joe Tropea and Chris Becker, Maryland Historical Society.

We would like to recognize the devoted JEA alumni who have preserved and generously shared with us their photos, memories, and memorabilia. Thanks to Bernie Cohen, Robert Goldstein, and Rae and Harry Rossen.

Voices of Lombard Street is the first Museum publication to appear since the death of Earl Pruce in May 2007 at age 97. Mr. Pruce's contribution to the preservation and documentation of Baltimore Jewish history truly cannot be measured. We dedicate this catalog to him.

The Editors

4

OPPOSITE: *East Fayette Street looking west toward the Shot Tower, circa 1926.*

JMM 1990.112.1

Foreword

BY DEBORAH R. WEINER,
ANITA KASSOF,
& AVI Y. DECTER

Lombard Street has been a touchstone for generations of Baltimore Jews, first as a center of community life and then as a locus of collective memory. Numerous families can trace their roots to the bustling East Baltimore immigrant neighborhood that surrounded Lombard Street. After they moved away, many returned each week to purchase traditional foods and soak up the old-world atmosphere. Even for Jews whose families never actually lived in "the old neighborhood," coming down to Lombard Street to shop was like "returning" to an ethnic past perhaps not directly experienced.

But Lombard Street is more than an icon of Baltimore's Jewish past. Through the years, the area has also been home to Italian Americans, African Americans, and a variety of others. They mingled on Lombard Street along with shoppers from across the city who came for the bargains, the fresh-killed chickens, and the camaraderie offered by storeowners who bantered with their customers and knew them by name.

Today, three delis and the campus of the Jewish Museum of Maryland, with its two historic synagogues, are the only physical reminders of the neighborhood's Jewish past. To say that the area has seen many changes would be an understatement. The recent redevelopment of the neighborhood, featuring blocks of brand-new rowhouses that echo the housing stock of the old immigrant enclave, has inspired us to focus renewed attention on our surroundings. *Voices of Lombard Street,* a major Museum initiative that includes an exhibition, educational and public programs, and this publication, explores the many meanings of Lombard Street and the history of our neighborhood.

Since the beginning of this project, it has been a challenge to identify a consistent name for this place. From the eighteenth century to today, the area has been known as "Jones Town," "Oldtown," "East End," "Jewtown," "the projects," "Jonestown," "Albemarle Square," or simply, "East Baltimore." Lombard Street is the common thread running through the neighborhood's checkered past. Identifying an entire enclave by the name of its most famous street, though, risks neglecting the varied, nuanced, and colorful history of the place as a whole. We have therefore looked beyond Lombard Street to the surrounding blocks where people lived, worked, played, and worshipped. From crowded tenements to twelve-story high rises, from public baths to Yiddish theaters, we have attempted to capture life in a "starter neighborhood" that was home to several generations of newcomers from Europe and the American South.

Through it all, Lombard Street remained—and perhaps again will become—the heartbeat of the neighborhood, the public square where people found common ground. Amidst the polarizing forces of city life, Lombard Street allowed people to engage in the shared humanity that is the best part of the urban experience. For that reason, it deserves our special attention.

Our authors have come together to create a catalog that explores in

depth the issues raised in the Museum's *Voices of Lombard Street* exhibition. While our gallery gives prominence to the "voices" of the people who lived or worked around Lombard Street—telling the story of the neighborhood largely through their words—the catalog gives us the opportunity to present commentary based on a wide range of sources and informed by recent scholarship, accompanied by powerful images that deepen our understanding of the topics that the essays address.

Researching and documenting the history of this remarkable neighborhood has been a joy. We have had the pleasure of talking with dozens of former and current residents, scholars, and our colleagues here at the Museum. We thank them for their consideration and encouragement, and we hope that this publication reflects their thoughtfulness as well as the lives lived in this landmark place.

Harry Tulkoff on Lombard Street, circa 1965.
Courtesy of Suzy Vogelhut, JMM 1992.189.4

7

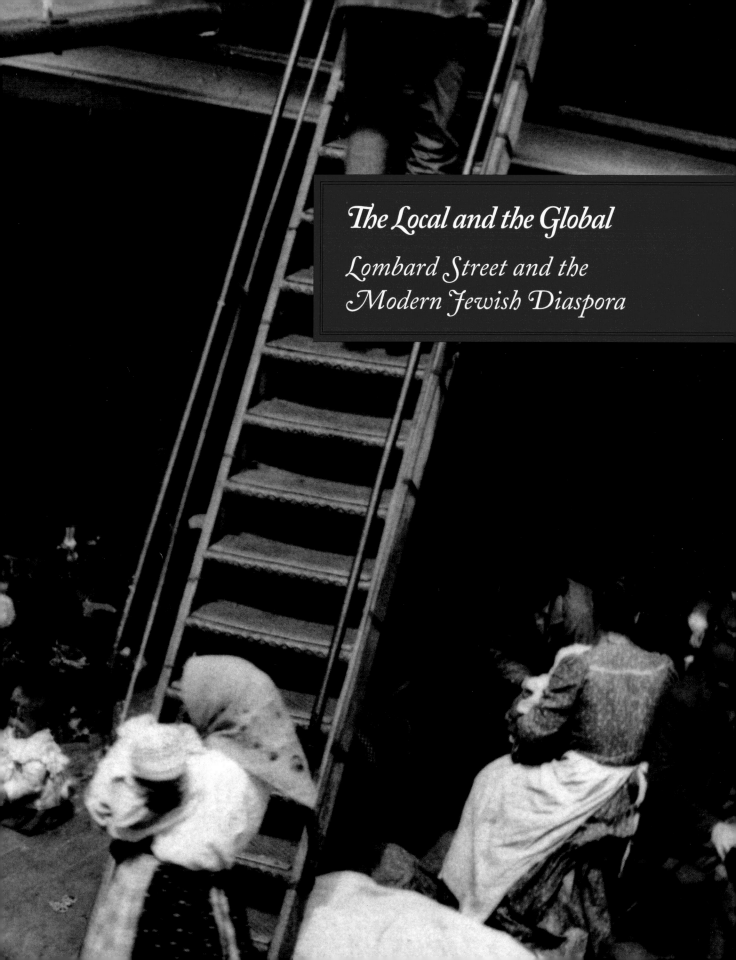

The Local and the Global

Lombard Street and the
Modern Jewish Diaspora

The Local and the Global: Lombard Street and the Modern Jewish Diaspora

BY HASIA DINER

Modern Jewish history, despite its cataclysmic political events and sweeping cultural transformations, can be seen as a profoundly local story. In the countless cities and towns where women and men made their homes and constructed their communities, they most intimately lived their lives as Jews. Here in their enclaves, they worked and congregated, worshipped and recreated, bought and sold, cooked, ate, slept, grew up, argued, did the laundry, schooled and raised their children. They also partook of the offerings of the larger society. Ultimately, they left their usually poor, congested areas for other, usually better, places to live.

Wherever they made their homes, Jews recognized themselves as belonging to a transnational people to whom they maintained connections and bore responsibilities. Yet, their local settings shaped them. In those settings they provided for their basic needs and found ways to give meaning to their lives. They experimented with new ideas about Jewish identity and culture partly in response to their experiences at the local level, where they interacted with a variety of other people—non-Jews, both members of the dominant society and other immigrants with whom they often lived in close proximity.

Immigration provides a key context for understanding the powerful influence of local places and the dramatic history of Jewish community formation in the modern era. In the great century of migration, what historians have dubbed "the long nineteenth century," from 1820 through the early 1920s, one-third of Europe's Jews—some three million people—took to the oceans, emigrating out of long-settled Jewish communities. Motivated largely by economic forces, young men and women on the move launched a major upheaval in Jewish life, shifting the locus of the Jewish people from Europe to the United States, where about 85 to 90 percent resettled. They ended up in other places as well, creating Jewish neighborhoods across several continents.

The waves of migration out of the old world started in Western and Central Europe and spread gradually eastward, for Jews as well as for a vast flood of other Europeans. In the 1820s the exodus hailed primarily from Bavaria and the Rhineland, moving in time to the eastern parts of Germany, particularly Posen, the formerly Polish province annexed by Prussia in the late eighteenth century. From Posen, the migration shifted gradually to Bohemia and Hungary. By the 1870s, migration came heavily from the eastern part of the Austro-Hungarian Empire, especially Galicia, and had begun to gather force in the area encompassing the Russian Empire's Jewish Pale of Settlement, starting with Lithuania. By the first decade of the twentieth century it spread through Poland and moved southeast through the Pale, to White Russia, Moldavia, and Ukraine.

The massive migration of Jews out of Europe left its mark on the lives of those who stayed behind. The exodus of such an enormous chunk of the

Hasia Diner, Ph.D., is the Paul S. and Sylvia Steinberg Professor of American Jewish History; Professor of Hebrew and Judaic Studies; and Director of the Goldstein-Goren Center for American Jewish History at New York University.

OVERLEAF: *Immigrants on the deck of the steamship* Kaiser Wilhelm der Grosse, *circa 1902.*

Courtesy of the Steamship Historical Society of America

10

Jewish population, particularly its youth, reshaped the economic and demographic profile of community life. Jews who remained in their home countries also transformed themselves by moving from small towns to pursue growing economic opportunities in big cities. In Europe, shtetl Jews became urbanites and they, like those who set sail from the ports of Rotterdam, Hamburg, and Bremen, encountered new cultural forms and ideas.

But immigration abroad proved to be more transformative, as Jews from Central and Eastern Europe discovered for themselves a series of new worlds. Wherever economic opportunities beckoned, they moved, planting Jewish outposts in the British Isles, the Americas, South Africa, and Australia. In these places, European Jews took their first step towards becoming American Jews, Canadian Jews, Australian Jews, South African Jews, Irish Jews, Cuban Jews, and the like.

Details of the migration shed light on the kinds of communities Jews would build in the various places they would eventually claim as their spaces. Jews tended, first and foremost, to be permanent emigrants. Although they maintained contact with family and townspeople who did not make the

Ella Rudick and her children, Jennie, Harry, Rose, Mannie, Lou, and Mike in Dublin, Ireland, 1912.

JMM 1988.209.53

Lombard Street, 1880s.

Courtesy of the Ross J. Kelbaugh Collection,
JMM 1988.226.5c

move, few chose to return to Europe. This fact tells us much about how they would react to their new homes. Since they did not intend to go back, they quickly went about the business of setting up communal structures to sustain Jewish life as they began to acquire the skills necessary to succeed in their chosen lands. The permanence of the migration meant that men and women tended to migrate in equal numbers (if not at the same time—husbands often came in advance of wives and children). In contrast, members of many other immigrant groups intended to return to their places of origin once they had acquired money. Italians and Greeks, for example, manifested high rates of return migration, and their migrations developed as male-heavy movements, with women, children, and the elderly remaining in the old country.

The United States was the most sought after destination for Jews as well as for other immigrant groups, and many who settled elsewhere hoped to make the move to America eventually. Regardless of their destinations, settling into a new land meant building a Jewish community, replete with local institutions, local practices, and local variations on universal Jewish themes. Like all other immigrants, Jews tended to go to places where fellow townspeople and family had gone first and where they had set up the rudiments of family and group life. Above all, they went to those countries, regions, and cities where economic opportunities could be found.

The first groups of Jews who left Central Europe in the 1820s migrated in relatively small numbers. They clustered together in their new homes, but did not have a large enough presence to transform their neighborhoods into obvious Jewish spaces. After the 1870s, the pace of migration picked up dramatically and the much greater movement out of Eastern Europe meant that Jewish newcomers could literally take over whole streets and sections in their destination cities. These all-encompassing Jewish neighborhoods, wherever they existed, shared many features. The similarities among them made for a global Jewish immigrant experience.

A Global View of the Jewish Immigrant Neighborhood

Because of the densely economic underpinnings of the migration, Jews who left Eastern Europe settled almost exclusively in cities, no matter where they landed. During that rapidly industrializing era, urban centers provided the greatest possibilities for making a living and enhancing in the long term the quality of their lives. And the bigger the city, the more Jews flocked to it. In every country they went to, the largest Jewish enclave developed in the largest city. New York, London, Buenos Aires, Havana, Toronto, Dublin, Glasgow, and Johannesburg became the dominant Jewish population centers in their respective countries, with secondary communities forming in second-tier cities such as Baltimore and Chicago, Leeds and Manchester, Limerick and Edinburgh. Jewish immigrants seemed to claim cities as their natural habitat and in fact became, in the eyes of their non-Jewish countrymen, over-associated with urban life.

Although few Jews migrated in organized groups, they saw themselves as part of a collectivity that went about the process of constructing community wherever they found themselves. The desire to live in proximity to those who shared their histories, identities, languages, religion, and values meant that Jewish immigrants clustered in enclaves that basically resembled one another, no matter where they were located.

For sure, place mattered, and each Jewish community had its own history, each worth telling in its own context. After all, what Jews did, and what happened to them, reflected the on-the-ground realities of the various societies in which their neighborhoods existed. They had to negotiate different sets of circumstances in order to achieve integration. Each city had its distinctive economic base. Each supported its own mosaic of ethnic groups and each, its idiosyncratic religious landscape. Each city and nation had its specific political structures. In every place they settled, Jews adapted to the particular pressures and unique opportunities exerted by the host culture. Each Jewish community, therefore, reflected the larger local environment, making each a universe of its own.

Jewish communities, for example, which formed in cities with large and complex immigrant populations of Italian, Polish, German, Irish, or Chinese newcomers, evolved differently than did those communities that developed in places with few or no other immigrants. Jewish immigrants in Dublin, Johannesburg, and Glasgow met and interacted with other poor people. But their new neighbors did not for the most part come from abroad, speak other foreign languages, or need to learn how to navigate the dominant culture from scratch. Jewish immigrants in American cities such as Baltimore, on the other hand, shared the immigrant experience and, oftentimes, space and institutions (such as public schools) with others equally "green" and just as far from the American mainstream as they.

Some Jewish immigrant communities, like Baltimore's, arose in cities that were legally segregated by color. The immigrants who flocked to Maryland's largest city arrived over the course of a century that witnessed the flourishing and then demise of slavery, followed by the imposition of a system that mandated the separation of African Americans from whites in schooling, public accommodations, and other arenas. The fact that Jews had the full privileges of "whiteness" from their first days in their new homes mattered more profoundly for Jews in Baltimore than, for example, those who settled in Chicago, Pittsburgh, or Boston—let alone Belfast or London, where racial preoccupations did not color social and political life.

But for all the distinctive features of each individual community, in the most profound sense, one Jewish neighborhood could very well stand in for another. Indeed, when surveying the histories of the many Jewish immigrant enclaves around the world, their likenesses trump their differences. Linguistic, political, economic, and cultural circumstances varied from Baltimore to

13

Yitzhak and Bessie Dubinksy with their children, Moishe, Chassa, and Ruchel, circa 1891, around the time of their immigration to Baltimore.

Gift of Marian E. Rubin, JMM 1987.27.1

Lombard Street, circa 1930.

Belfast, Montreal to Mexico City, New York to London. But when it came to the texture of Jewish immigrant life, similarities bound them together.

The economic marginality of the immigrant generation molded family and community life, whether the locale was Baltimore's Lombard Street, New York's Lower East Side, Washington, D.C.'s Half Street, Chicago's Maxwell Street, Montreal's St. Urbain Street, Havana's Calle Luz, Dublin's Clanbrassill Street, or London's Stepney neighborhood. Pushed out of Europe largely by difficult economic conditions, immigrants were drawn to the possibility that in these new places they could make a decent living. While communal rhetoric both during and after the migration emphasized the flight of Jews from Eastern European pogroms and other vicious outbreaks of anti-Jewish violence, economic matters in fact weighed heavily upon them. They left a world of diminishing economic possibilities and increasing impoverishment. Most migrated in order to contemplate a livable future.

The drive to make a living shaped Jewish immigrant neighborhoods. Regardless of the city, Jews could be found as peddlers hawking goods on the street and as small shopkeepers selling all manner of goods, living above or behind their stores. Each city had its subset of vendors who sold kosher food and other items necessary to maintaining a Jewish way of life. Jewish-owned stores essentially made the Jewish enclaves. The main commercial streets served as the spines of their neighborhoods. In the shops and on the streets, Jews met, socialized, and interacted with one another, blending the entrepreneurial and the communal spheres.

The fact that shopkeeping and housekeeping existed side by side for families around the world solidified the tight bond between Jewish business and daily Jewish life. Fusing work and home extended the hours a store could stay open and helped make the commercial infrastructure organic to the life of the community. Histories and memoirs of Jewish life in places as disparate as Dublin, Havana, and Baltimore tell this same story and make this very prosaic detail a common feature of the global Jewish narrative.

The involvement of immigrant Jews in garment making proved equally unifying, leaving a profound mark on Jewish history worldwide. In each locale, Jews made a living in the clothing industry, making it their particular métier. Small workshops commonly referred to as "sweatshops" appeared in the early years of the life histories of all Jewish enclaves, and like small stores, sweatshops doubled as employers' homes, enabling immigrant Jews to live and work in the same neighborhood. In clothing factories the world over, Jewish workers labored for Jewish employers. This affected how workers organized and how they articulated their demands upon their bosses. Their shared Jewishness limited the bosses' ability to ignore completely workers' calls for better wages and better conditions. Union organizing by the men and women who worked in the needle trades dominated community life. The public spaces of Jewish neighborhoods, the streets, squares, parks, and meeting halls throbbed with the sounds of Jewish workers demanding rights from Jewish employers.

Moreover, the making of clothing required little in the way of start-up capital and supported many small-scale enterprises. It was one of the few

15

Lombard Street, circa 1930.
Gift of Jack Lerner, JMM 1998.17.1

industries where a worker could realistically imagine becoming a manufacturer. Jewish neighborhood life took much of its tempo from widespread involvement in garment making and from the expectation, often fulfilled, of economic mobility.

Regardless of where in the world they popped up, Jewish enclaves resounded with Yiddish as the language of the streets and the home. While over time the local language, whether English, Spanish, or French, could be heard as well, in the years that these neighborhoods housed substantial immigrant populations, Yiddish served as their *lingua franca*. People shopped in it, worked in it, and lived in it. It rang through the city streets. Over time the words, phrases, and sentences of the dominant language were folded into Yiddish, as immigrant entrepreneurs interacted with non-Jewish customers, and as children of immigrants attended state-sponsored schools, acquiring the tools to "make it" in the world outside their Yiddish-inflected streets.

Yiddish also served as a global medium of information. The development of Yiddish newspapers by the end of the nineteenth century meant that residents of Jewish neighborhoods learned about the world in this language. The Jewish streets became places where newsstands displayed the Yiddish written word, reinforcing certain public spaces as overtly Jewish.

Some immigrants realized that Yiddish could serve as a vehicle for political education. Socialists in particular, around the global Jewish world, sought to refashion Jews into class-conscious activists. They helped develop a Yiddish press that conveyed a particular political message. Regardless of where the enclave happened to be, socialists also played a crucial role in shaping Jewish trade unions and in creating mutual aid societies and other organizations that melded political work with Jewish sociability.

Yiddish enjoyed tremendous popularity as a language of entertainment. Large Yiddish-speaking neighborhoods all over the world supported theatrical venues. While New York, Buenos Aires, Chicago, and Montreal, for example, had their own Jewish theater companies and even full theatrical districts, smaller cities waited for traveling troupes to come to them. Actors from New York brought productions to Havana and Dublin, just as they staged their plays in Milwaukee and Seattle. But whether the city had enough immigrant Jews to sustain a full-blown Yiddish theatrical world or if they had to depend on exports from larger communities, the quality of life in the neighborhood took part of its shape from the ability of Jews to entertain one another in their own language.

In addition to the tight conjoining of work, residence, and social life, Jewish neighborhoods resembled one another in their support of Jewish institutions. Wherever they settled, Jews banded together to fulfill their religious obligations, clustering into congregations both formal and informal. These congregations, with names that identified themselves as, for example, "*anshe*" or "*hevre*"—"men of" or "fellowship of"—often

17

TOP: *Yiddish stage actress Bessie Thomaschevsky met her future husband Boris when he performed in Baltimore, and the pair went on to tour nationally.* JMM CP8.2007.1

BOTTOM: *Poster for "A Lost Fortune" at the Orpheum Theatre in Baltimore, circa 1910.* JMM K2000.18.2

OPPOSITE: *A sweatshop on Lloyd Street in East Baltimore, circa 1915.*

Gift of Caroline H. Bernstein and Helen K. Silverberg, JMM 1991.24.3a

Founding members of the Amalgamated Clothing Workers Union, 1915.

Gift of Rosalie Wolfson, JMM 1990.91.1a

splintered along the lines of European place of origin. The larger the Jewish population, the more congregations cropped up and the more specific the *anshes* and *hevras* could be to places of origin.

In their religious gathering places, men worshipped and socialized with others from the towns and regions of Europe they had abandoned. Typically, congregation members at first rented spaces (often churches no longer in use) to hold their services. Sometime they moved into synagogues previously occupied by Jewish congregations whose members had departed the neighborhood and could now afford grander accommodations. At times, immigrant congregations built their own lofty structures. Whether located in new buildings or recycled ones, synagogues dominated the landscape of the immigrant enclave. Immigrant life took much of its tone from the passage of Jewish time, Sabbath to Sabbath, holiday to holiday. Yet immigrant Jews, everywhere, did not necessarily agree that Judaism, with its prescribed laws and ritual practices, constituted the key aspect of Jewishness. Enclaves all over the world supported various ideologies and factions that espoused radically different ideas about the meaning of Jewish identity in the modern world. In addition to Orthodoxy, Socialists, Zionists, and anarchists represented only a few of the most organized constituencies within the Jewish quarters. Each ideology in turn built its own institutions and launched publications to rally supporters. The intense debate that raged over matters of Jewish politics and culture spanned the globe and made Jewish immigrant neighborhoods into battlegrounds of ideas. The struggle for ideological supremacy within the immigrant enclave heightened the intensity and drama of community life.

Religious obligations encompassed much more than just worship. Following the traditional imperative to help one another, Jews in every country created a string of institutions such as free loan societies, orphanages, old-age homes, medical clinics, and burial societies. They formed *landsmanshaftn,* organizations of townspeople from particular European hometowns. These provided medical care, unemployment compensation, sickness and burial benefits, as well as fellowship and leisure activities. Such aid societies did not really constitute "charity." Jews created them because their tradition mandated that they do so. Also, they recognized that in the vagaries of life, they too might some day be in need of assistance. The existence in their community of a fund that helped unemployed workers, an institution that took in orphans, or an association that made interest-free loans to help members "get back on their feet" functioned as a kind of insurance policy against the ever-present possibility of reversal of circumstance. The building of Jewish community life around the provision of assistance was a transnational Jewish pattern, varying little from place to place. The fact that the same kinds of assistance knit each community together demonstrated the fundamental importance of Jewish mutuality.

In addition to family economic crises, immigrant Jewish neighborhoods bred a range of social problems that accompanied both poverty and the

generational chasm between old-country parents and new-world children. Poor housing, overcrowded living spaces, dirt, and diseases ran rampant. Each community had to confront issues of crime, prostitution, and marital desertion.

In many places, Jewish enclaves could receive assistance for these universal woes from beyond their community's boundaries. Jews who immigrated from Eastern Europe starting in the late nineteenth century often settled in cities that housed a smaller, older, more established, and more affluent class of Jews. These assimilated Jews had either themselves been immigrants in decades past, or their parents or grandparents had arrived a generation or two earlier. Having already gone through the process of immigration, settlement, adaptation, and integration into the larger society, they played an important role in the new immigrant neighborhood.

Most obviously and most significantly, the already-established Jewish community created and/or funded institutions that paved the way for the later immigrants' new world journeys. They opened hospitals, schools, camps, and training institutions to relieve some of the worst of the suffering, boost immigrants' workplace skills, and usher them onto the path of modernization by exposing them to new ideas. Their philanthropic projects gave immigrants and their children access to swimming pools, gymnasia, fresh air, and concert halls. In their settlement houses, immigrants learned art, cooking, sewing, how to acquire citizenship, and the language of the land. All these undertakings addressed, in one way or another, the question of how newcomers could gain the knowledge necessary to negotiate the terrain of their chosen land. Perhaps less obviously, the appearance of these "do-gooders" provided Eastern European immigrants—and particularly their children—with role models of Jews who comfortably functioned in the larger society. That modeling took place wherever immigrant Jews set up their many neighborhoods.

The middle-class Jews who came into immigrant neighborhoods and

TOP: *Benjamin Klasmer conducts the Jewish Educational Alliance Orchestra in East Baltimore, 1919.*

Gift of Blanche Cohen, JMM 1977.24.1

BOTTOM: *Passover seder at the Hebrew Home for the Incurables in East Baltimore, circa 1920.*

Gift of Earl Pruce, JMM 1985.90.9

19

dispensed their largesse did so from a mix of motives. Indeed, some immigrants expressed irritation and resentment at what they perceived as the haughtiness their benefactors displayed to them, the befuddled newcomers. But the presence of these more established Jews proved invaluable in fostering adaptation to the immigrants' new homes, be they in Baltimore or Buenos Aires. And in all the places where Eastern European Jews became objects of the philanthropy of their more affluent coreligionists, the first native-born generation from the later group succeeded well enough and quickly enough that within a few decades they took over control of the Jewish community.

Moving Up and Out of the Old Neighborhood

Eastern European Jews settled in massive numbers in their new cities and left their impress upon the cityscape in ways that previous immigrant generations could not. But their neighborhoods, despite their size, density, and the richness of their institutions, functioned as giant sieves. Immigrants came in, settled down, and moved out to other sections of the city. Successive waves of Jewish newcomers took their places, settling in and continuing to make the streets of East Baltimore, Dublin's Little Jerusalem, or London's East End theirs.

This process came to an end for two reasons. First, wherever Jewish immigrants moved, they tended to experience steady economic mobility. They had no reason to stay in cramped and crowded quarters on Lombard Street, Maxwell Street, or the East End when they could rent or buy houses in greener and healthier areas of Baltimore, Chicago, or London. Second, national policies formulated in congresses and parliaments exerted a decisive influence. Immigration restrictions imposed in Great Britain in the first decade of the twentieth century and in the United States in the early 1920s brought an end to the era of the great migration. New waves of Jewish newcomers no longer arrived in crowded immigrant districts to take the place of upwardly mobile Jews, occupy their apartments or synagogues, or patronize their commercial corridors. Formerly Jewish streets became home to other poor people—in the case of many American cities, African-American migrants from the rural South.

This did not mean, however, that in one broad stroke these places ceased to be Jewish spaces. Jews remained connected to their old neighborhoods. Older members of the community lingered on, as did poorer Jews. Synagogues remained for years after the bulk of their members moved elsewhere. Merchants also stayed on for a while longer. Jews who had moved away tended to return to purchase Jewish goods, ritual objects, and most importantly, traditional foods. Trips back to the old immigrant quarter to buy distinctively Jewish food made the neighborhoods objects of nostalgia.

Retrospectively, these places became the stuff of history and memory. When Jews set about the task of constructing their communal, family, and personal narratives about the past, they focused in on the details of life in the

Park Heights Avenue, north of Park Circle, circa 1940s. Many Eastern European Jews moved to this part of northwest Baltimore after leaving the old neighborhood.

Courtesy of Stanford C. Reed, JMM 1987.19.28

20

neighborhoods where they had once lived. Where physical traces existed to prove that once upon a time, Jews had occupied particular spaces, the immigrants' descendants found ways to enshrine the past. By the late 1960s, as they became interested in tracing their roots, they started putting up markers, creating museums and other historical projects to remind themselves about the immigrant era. They looked to their pasts and told their stories from the street level, describing where they had come from, in part to explain where they eventually went.

Each Jewish city has its own Lombard Street and each Lombard Street has its distinctive and notable "firsts." Each has its roster of important individuals who gave money, created organizations, and inspired followers. Each Jewish community in the United States and indeed throughout the diaspora shares such a history and harbors memories of such an area of first settlement. And each history deserves to be told, whether in popular books, scholarly works, exhibitions, oral history projects, or documentary films. Each history tells a specific tale of migration, adaptation, community building, and mobility. Since each community nurtured its own residents, they and their descendants rightly should see their forbears and themselves as historic actors.

The Jewish women and men who built up and lived in East Baltimore had stories worth telling for their own sake, for what they say about how ordinary people lived their lives. But when thinking about the history of Baltimore's old Jewish neighborhood in conjunction with the global stories collected from around the Jewish "new world," the former denizens of Lombard Street can be seen as having participated in a profound social upheaval that left its mark on Jewish history. East Baltimore has a unique story to tell, but it also serves as one of many exemplars of the massive Jewish population movement from east to west, which constituted a crucial chapter in the history of the Jewish people.

TOP: *The Jewish Museum of Maryland campus with the B'nai Israel synagogue (1876) on the right.*

Photo by Carl Caruso, courtesy of Historic Jonestown, Inc.

BOTTOM: *The Lloyd Street Synagogue after restoration, circa 1965. Today, the Synagogue is owned and operated by the Jewish Museum of Maryland.*

Gift of Suzy (Sarah) Vogelhut, JMM 1992.189.6

A Different Kind of Neighborhood

*Central European Jews and
the Origins of Jewish East Baltimore*

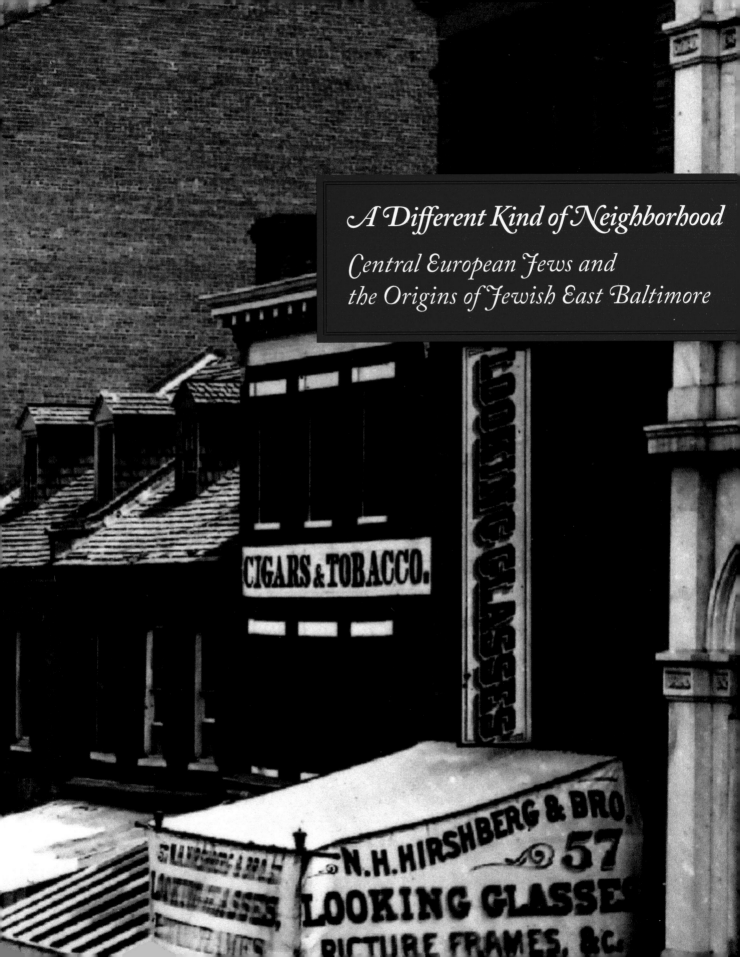

CIGARS & TOBACCO.

LOOKING GLASSES

N.H. HIRSHBERG & BRO. 57
LOOKING GLASSES
PICTURE FRAMES, &c.

A Different Kind of Neighborhood: Central European Jews and the Origins of Jewish East Baltimore

BY ERIC L. GOLDSTEIN

Eric Goldstein, Ph.D., is Associate Professor in the Department of History and the Institute for Jewish Studies at Emory University.

OVERLEAF: *Hanover Street, West Baltimore, with Temple Oheb Shalom in center of block, circa 1872.*

Courtesy of the Ross J. Kelbaugh Collection, JMM 1988.226.2a

*I*n one of the more symbolic scenes in Sidney Nyburg's novel of Baltimore Jewish life, *The Chosen People* (1917), the protagonist, a young Reform rabbi named Philip Graetz, goes walking through the center of East Baltimore, the main district for the city's Eastern European Jews. Though an American-born Jew of German parentage who had only recently arrived in Baltimore, Graetz strongly hoped to encourage a sense of unity between the newer immigrants who lived in this neighborhood and the wealthier and more acculturated members of his own "uptown" congregation. As he walked along past the "ugly houses" and the "tiny meat and grocery shops," he remembered something that helped him see these unkempt surroundings as somewhat less forbidding. The voice of one of his older congregants came to him, explaining how he had been born in this neighborhood and how many of the "families now most influential and affluent in the Jewish community had lived there . . . before the flood tide of immigration from Russia and Poland had begun." If his recollection of the old man's story allowed him to feel a connection to the East Baltimore "ghetto," his thoughts soon drifted back to the differences between the two communities as he thought about "how strange and unfamiliar" the neighborhood would appear "to the ghost of some thrifty, German-Jewish housewife . . . should she feel moved in the dead of night to visit once more."[1]

As Nyburg's novel suggests, Baltimore Jews of Central European descent (popularly referred to as "German" Jews) were at least faintly aware in 1917 that the streets of East Baltimore, despite having been transformed into an enclave for newer immigrants, had once been among their own haunts. Today, although the dominant image of East Baltimore emphasizes the legacy of immigrants from Russia and Poland whose influence can still be detected on Lombard Street's Corned Beef Row, local Jewish historical consciousness continues to affirm that East Baltimore has an older history stretching back to the "German" period.[2] The story of neighborhood succession from Central European to Eastern European Jews is a key part of the narrative told by docents at the two historic synagogues that now form part of the Jewish Museum of Maryland complex, both of which were built by Central European Jews in the mid nineteenth century and were subsequently taken over by Eastern European immigrants who arrived in large numbers beginning in the 1880s. The Lloyd Street Synagogue, used after 1905 by the Volhynian Jewish congregation Shomrei Mishmeres Hakodesh, had originally been built in 1845 by the Baltimore Hebrew Congregation, composed of German and Dutch Jews, who occupied the structure until 1889. Down the street, the building known as the "Russishe shul," which was occupied by B'nai Israel Congregation beginning in 1895, was originally built by another congregation of Central European Jews, Chizuk Amuno, in 1876.[3]

If the early "German" Jewish presence in East Baltimore is a recognized part of the historical record, however, very little is known about the actual

texture of Jewish life in that district before the 1880s, or the extent to which it resembled or anticipated the Jewish atmosphere that characterized the area during the early twentieth century. What was the relationship between the East Baltimore of the Eastern European Jews and that of their Central European predecessors?

First, we can say with certainty that the area east of the Jones Falls (see map, inside front cover) would likely have attracted Eastern European Jews arriving in Baltimore from the 1880s regardless of the earlier Jewish presence there, just as it attracted Italian, Greek, Polish, and Lithuanian immigrants looking to find their niche in the urban landscape. In fact, because Eastern European Jews vastly outnumbered their Central European predecessors, they eventually occupied a much larger swath of East Baltimore than did the earlier settlers, who concentrated themselves mainly in the several-block area east of the Jones Falls then known as Oldtown.[4] By the 1920s, Jewish East Baltimore had spread out much further east, past Broadway to the area around Patterson Park. Still, despite the divergences, it is quite evident

East Fayette Street, late 1800s.
JMM 1988.117.1

B'nai Israel Congregation (formerly the Chizuk Amuno Congregation) on Lloyd Street, circa 1910.

Jewish Museum of Maryland

that the presence of earlier Central European Jewish immigrants decisively shaped the pattern of settlement for the Eastern European newcomers. It was no coincidence that the streets on which Polish and Russian Jews initially sought out housing and places to establish their synagogues and communal institutions were the same ones long occupied by "German" Jews. Although by the turn of the twentieth century the district centered near the corner of Baltimore and Lloyd Streets had become known as the heart of the Eastern European Jewish "ghetto," this area had already been given a Jewish flavor by Jews from Central Europe who had arrived there several decades earlier.

As important as Central European Jews were in establishing a Jewish presence in East Baltimore during the mid nineteenth century, however, their impact on the area and their experience of it as a "neighborhood" was decidedly different from that of the later immigrants from Eastern Europe. Because the two groups differed significantly in terms of their size and demographic makeup, their occupational profile, their level of acculturation, and their integration into the non-Jewish world, their relationship to city space also differed. Moreover, Baltimore in general was a different city in 1900 than it had been in 1850 or 1870, and areas such as East Baltimore took on a different character as the city's population grew, the locations of industry changed, and Baltimoreans became more divided according to class, race, and ethnicity. Memories of East Baltimore as a district thickly populated with Jews and with streets lined with ritual slaughterers, Jewish bakeries, and Jewish institutions may represent the reality of neighborhood life as it existed during the early twentieth century, but they have little resemblance to what life was like there for Central European Jews of the previous generation. As this essay will demonstrate, Central European Jews never became as dominant an element in their East Baltimore surroundings as Eastern European Jews later would, nor did the area ever become the single most important neighborhood for Baltimore's Jews in the period before the Eastern European influx. Instead, it was a hub mainly for Jewish religious congregations. Its role as a central location for other types of Jewish institutions was much less important, and it was only one of the many residential districts where Jews lived across the city during these years. Thus, while the earliest Jews in East Baltimore helped in many ways lay the groundwork for the dense Jewish neighborhood that came later, they could have hardly imagined such a world in their own day.

THE "SCATTERED OF ISRAEL"

In 1830, just four years after the Jews of Maryland acquired equal civil status under the state constitution with the passage of the "Jew Bill," the first Jewish congregation in Baltimore was chartered. Calling itself the Baltimore Hebrew Congregation, it also adopted a Hebrew name, Nidche Yisrael—the "scattered of Israel."[5] Though the Hebrew name was one used by other congregations across the globe to describe the plight of Jews in exile and their hope for redemption, the organizers of Baltimore Hebrew also intended it as a description of their own Jewish community, whose members were widely scattered across the entire city. In fact, in requesting their charter from the Maryland state legislature, they styled themselves "the scattered Israelites of the city of Baltimore."[6] The federal census taken the same year confirms this characterization, showing that Baltimore's thirty Jewish households were spread over ten of the city's twelve wards. Although there was a small concentration of Dutch and German Jews in Fells Point—at that time the main port for arriving immigrants—and another concentration of wealthy, mostly native-born Jews in the area around North Charles Street, two-thirds of the Jewish households conformed to no recognizable pattern of residential clustering.[7]

By 1840, when Baltimore's Jewish population had grown to about 1,000 souls, a pattern of dispersal across the city with some noticeable residential clustering had become more pronounced. In this respect, the city's Jewish community was similar to those in other American cities, where the emergence of sharply segregated Jewish quarters was still rare.[8] At a time when industrialization had not yet firmly taken hold in the United States, Jews were primarily occupied with trade and commerce and often lived at or near their places of business. Commercial success meant reaching out to customers of all backgrounds, so Jews lived wherever opportunities for trade were the best. This meant that they generally spread out to the city's various marketing centers rather than gathering in one principal area. Jews, however, were not alone among Baltimore's immigrants in lacking a central residential gathering point. Because all kinds of skilled and unskilled work was still performed on a local basis in the era before mechanization and mass transportation, nineteenth-century immigrants did not have the luxury of creating the large ethnic enclaves that later came to characterize the city. As demographer Joseph Garonzik explains of the foreign born in this period, occupational proximity was "higher on the head of household's list of priorities than ethnic residential proximity."[9]

With Baltimore Jews of the nineteenth century setting up home where they set up shop, the various Jewish residential clusters in the city quickly became synonymous with the major business districts. The two most significant concentrations of Jews could now be found in Fells Point and the downtown Centre Market area, which had been centers of trade in Baltimore since the eighteenth century and had attracted a significant number of Central European Jewish newcomers by the 1830s. Fells Point remained the port for arriving immigrants until just after the Civil War and was also the city's major shipping and ship-building center. After 1867, when many of these functions shifted to other parts of the harbor, Fells Point retained its importance as the location of light industries such as canning and packing, which thrived along the waterfront.[10] Jews settled mainly on Bond and Camden (later Fleet) Streets, and especially along Broadway surrounding the Broadway Market,

Samuel Kahn and his mother Amelia standing in front of Kahn's Store on Harrison Street, circa 1880.

Gift of Philip Kahn, Jr., JMM 1990.204.1

27

Centre Market, undated drawing.

Courtesy of the Enoch Pratt Free Library, Central Library/State Resource Center

Baltimore Street from Centre Market, circa 1850.

Courtesy of The Maryland Historical Society

where they found that they could sell goods to a steady flow of customers. Similar reasoning attracted Jews to the three-block strip between Baltimore and Pratt Streets known as Centre Market Space, which surrounded the Centre Market—Baltimore's oldest—on both sides.[11] Here, Jews selling clothing, boots, and shoes soon came to constitute a substantial proportion of the merchants. The most densely Jewish street in the neighborhood was Harrison Street, which ran north from the market and became home to dozens of Jewish-owned pawnshops, second-hand stores, and other fairly low-grade business enterprises.[12]

As Jewish immigration to Baltimore increased during the 1840s, Jewish business enterprises—and with them, residences—spread to other important commercial streets and districts. Gay Street, running north from the Centre Market area and then to the northeast across the Jones Falls, became a favorite area for Jewish-owned dry goods, millinery, and furniture stores. Like the two older Jewish hubs, Gay Street was also the location of a city market

Moses Millhauser and Sam Ullman standing outside Millhauser's Gay Street store.

Gift of Richard Millhauser, JMM 1991.133.2

house, the Belair Market. The Central European Jews who opened up shops nearby were the first of their group to venture into the area know as Oldtown, although during these early years Jews remained only in the northern part of the district near the market. West Baltimore Street, which was described by one observer as the city's "great promenade . . . containing many handsome shops and stores," also became a magnet for Jewish businesses, particularly higher-end dry goods emporiums and clothing establishments, which ran from the Centre Market area far into West Baltimore and spilled over onto surrounding streets.[13] A few blocks to the south, closer to the harbor, Pratt Street became a major location for the same type of Jewish-owned businesses, although there they extended only as far west as Eutaw Street.

Baltimore's Jewish residential patterns as they had emerged in the 1830s and 1840s reflected the strong priority of Central European Jewish immigrants to establish themselves in business and to create a solid economic foundation for their new lives in America. These patterns also reflected the success many immigrants enjoyed. Though not every Jew of this period went on to become a prominent clothing wholesaler or manufacturer, Baltimore Jews did find a welcoming environment that put few obstacles in their path to self-improvement and social mobility. Indeed, their ability to live and work in so many parts of the city demonstrated just how open the urban landscape was to them. If the dispersion of Baltimore Jews facilitated their fervent pursuit of economic opportunity, however, it was not as helpful in providing them with a sense of cohesion as a community. By 1845, many of Baltimore's Jewish immigrants began to think about ways to begin binding their scattered brothers and sisters more closely together.

A Different Kind of Jewish Neighborhood

The corner of Fleet and Bond Streets, circa 1930. The Baltimore Hebrew Congregation was located above the corner store from 1830 to 1832.

Courtesy of the Baltimore Hebrew Congregation Archives, JMM 1989.94.4a

In envisioning themselves as a community, Baltimore's Central European Jews had few expectations that they could live in a largely Jewish world. In addition to the economic considerations that kept Jews from living together in large enclaves, the size of Baltimore's Jewish population—like the American Jewish population as a whole during this period—was simply too small to produce residential areas composed mainly of Jews. Having peddled during their early years in America through remote areas in western Maryland, Pennsylvania, and the Eastern Shore, many of them knew the necessity of spreading out in order to make a living.[14] Moreover, before their arrival in this country, most Jewish immigrants of this period had lived in small towns and villages where modest clusters of Jews were surrounded by non-Jewish peasant populations.[15] Thus, although Baltimore Jews of the mid nineteenth century were spread out around the city, they enjoyed what most would have considered a high level of contact and interaction with other Jews.

Still, geographical dispersion did pose specific challenges that required creative solutions, as former village dwellers and countryside peddlers well knew. Because of their previous experiences, Central European Jews had become proficient at creating networks and relationships that transcended geography, providing a sense of community in the absence of a single Jewish gathering point.[16] It was precisely these skills that Baltimore's Jewish immigrants called upon in the 1840s in creating institutions that were accessible and could be shared by Jews living in different parts of the city.

As Baltimore's foreign-born Jews began to spread out during the 1830s to various parts of the city, one of the greatest challenges they faced was finding appropriate locations for their religious congregations. This was an especially pressing issue at a time when a significant proportion of Baltimore Jews still adhered to religious restrictions against riding on the Sabbath. All of the congregations founded before 1850 drew members from across the city and faced the dilemma of deciding in which Jewish residential cluster to locate. The oldest congregation, Baltimore Hebrew, moved its location several times, trying to find the place where it would best serve its diffuse flock. Starting out in Fells Point in 1830, it then rented a series of buildings just below the North Gay Street cluster. Later, from 1837 to 1845, the congregation worshipped in a rented house on Harrison Street. Shortly after Baltimore Hebrew left Fells Point, another synagogue, Oheb Israel (also known as the Fells Point Hebrew Friendship Congregation), sprang up there to serve the local population. It soon found, however, that its growing membership was highly mobile and that its location so far to the east was not as ideal as its founders had imagined. Har Sinai, Baltimore's first Reform congregation, also struggled with serving a diffuse membership, though in its case convenience was probably more at stake than issues surrounding Sabbath observance. The congregation held its first worship service in 1842 downtown on Baltimore Street, but then shifted to holding services across town, in the Fells Point home of Moses Hutzler.[17] During these years, all of these congregations met in temporary quarters, a factor that made it easier to avoid any final decision about the difficult choice of where to locate. By the mid 1840s, however, these three pioneer congregations had grown prosperous enough that they were finally able to sink permanent roots. As a result, they were pushed to find a solution to the problem of Baltimore's "scattered Israelites."

In 1845, Baltimore Hebrew Congregation became the first of the city's Jewish congregations to search for a new, permanent location for a synagogue. Instead of choosing one of the many Jewish clusters, the congregation's leaders decided to try a novel approach—locating the synagogue in a neighborhood populated by almost no Jews, but one that was located between the various Jewish population centers in an area that was accessible to all or most of them. The place they chose was the corner of Lloyd and Watson Streets, in the southern part of Oldtown. The Lloyd Street location proved ideal, since it was located right between the Fells Point and Centre Market/Harrison Street areas and just below the North Gay Street/Belair Market district. Though it was farther from West Pratt and Baltimore Streets, the trek from there was not impossible, especially since both thoroughfares eventually fed right into the neighborhood as they crossed the Jones Falls. Baltimore Hebrew's idea worked well, and three years later, in 1848, Oheb Israel Congregation, formerly of Fells Point, followed its lead and moved to Eden Street, just a few blocks to the east of the Lloyd Street Synagogue. The next year, Har Sinai built its new temple on High Street within a few blocks of the other two

This building housed the Hebrew Friendship Congregation (Oheb Israel) until it disbanded around 1902. The photo was taken around 1910, after the building had become home to Aitz Chaim, the "Eden Street Shul."

Jewish Museum of Maryland

TOP: *West Baltimore Street opposite Hanover Street, circa 1865.*

Gift of Joseph Wiesenfeld, JMM 1990.2.6d

BOTTOM: *Moses Wiesenfeld in the 1850s.*

Gift of Joseph Wiesenfeld, JMM 1990.2.12

congregations.[18] With the city's three Jewish congregations now located in close proximity to one another, a new kind of Jewish neighborhood had been born in the heart of East Baltimore, one that served as home to a number of synagogues but not to a significant number of Jews.

This anomalous status, however, did not continue for long. Meyer Hecht, whose father Samuel later became one of Baltimore's leading department store owners, recalled that when his family moved within a few blocks of the Lloyd Street synagogue in 1848 to open a store, "the neighborhood for a considerable distance was composed of native born people of American descent."[19] Confirming the paucity of Jews in the area, historian Michael S. Franch analyzed the Baltimore Hebrew Congregation's 1849 membership list to find that only 4 percent of member families lived within a quarter mile of the synagogue. Yet by 1860, the number had jumped to 27 percent, revealing that Jews were beginning to follow Baltimore Hebrew and its sister congregations to East Baltimore.[20] Jews had settled throughout the area, especially on the main thoroughfares linking East Baltimore with the city center—East Lombard, Pratt, and Baltimore Streets—as well as on Central Avenue and on the several streets running north from Fayette towards Gay Street.

This influx was a sign of the continuing good fortune of Baltimore's Jewish merchants, many of whom could now afford to live apart from their places of business. While a few Jews who moved into the area opened up groceries, tailor shops, and other modest enterprises there, by and large the neighborhood was treated as a convenient place from which to commute to one of the established Jewish business districts. In 1864, for example, the prominent clothier Moses Wiesenfeld lived at 111 East Baltimore Street and worked across the Jones Falls at 23-25 West Baltimore Street. Another clothier, Seligman Bernei, traveled easily from his East Baltimore Street home to his large store on the Centre Market Space, while Mendel Herzberg, a resident of East Lombard Street, lived only about five blocks from his notions store at 175 North Gay Street.[21]

Although East Baltimore's synagogues encouraged Jewish residents from other parts of the city to locate there in the decades after 1845, the area never succeeded in becoming what one might call the principal Jewish district of the city. The influx did not overwhelm the neighborhood or change its character significantly, with Jews always remaining a minority—as they were in the other hubs—among German and Irish immigrants and native-born Americans. Neither did the new East Baltimore cluster threaten to eclipse the other areas of Jewish settlement. Most Jews in the city were happy to have a central place to attend synagogue, but otherwise preferred to remain where they were. They did not look to East Baltimore as the place to get their kosher food, since kosher meat remained available at no fewer than six markets spread across the city.[22] Not only did the other Jewish clusters retain their strength, but during the 1850s and 1860s two additional Jewish residential areas emerged, one in South Baltimore along Hanover and South Charles Streets, where many of the clothing and dry goods merchants of West Pratt and Baltimore Streets began to gather, and the other in the vicinity of Lexington and Howard Streets, which was emerging as Baltimore's leading apparel district. [23]

The draw of these new areas was their social prominence, as they became gathering places for a rising generation of Jewish clothing manufacturers, department store owners, and professionals. Aaron Friedenwald, who had originally moved with his family from Fells Point to East Baltimore, headed for the west side in 1868 because he felt it would be a more appropriate place for the medical practice he was establishing.[24] For similar reasons, the west side also became an increasingly attractive venue for the social activities of the Jewish community. The Concordia Association, a German social club made up largely of Jewish members, originally met at the corner of East Fayette Street and Central Avenue, but in 1864 it moved to a beautiful new opera house at the corner of German and Eutaw Streets.[25]

Even synagogues sprang up in the new clusters. Congregation Oheb Shalom, founded in a North Gay Street hall in 1853, decided to build its permanent place of worship on Hanover Street rather than in East Baltimore, while Howard Street became the location of the orthodox Shearith Israel, as well as some other short-lived congregations.[26] Thus, as the nineteenth century pressed on, Baltimore's Central European Jews showed no signs of ceasing their spread across the city. When Abraham Brafman, a native of Bavaria and a founding member of Oheb Shalom, bought a house on Lexington Street from a local financier, the seller revealed that he was selling

Carte-de-visite of Oheb Shalom, Hanover Street, circa 1870.

Courtesy of the Ross J. Kelbaugh Collection, JMM 1997.71.2

Aaron Friedenwald.

Gift of Judith Harris, JMM 1991.129.39

The German-English School at Fayette and Green Streets in West Baltimore, late 1890s. Both Jews and gentiles attended the school.

Gift of Judith Senker Wise, JMM 1985.51.1

to get away from Jews, but he did not know where in Baltimore he could go to get away from them. "That's easy," replied Brafman, "move to the Penitentiary—you won't find any Jews there!"[27]

Despite all the forces detracting from East Baltimore's dominance among Jewish clusters in the city during the nineteenth century, it did remain a special and distinct area in a few important ways. Although synagogues had begun to emerge in other parts of Baltimore by the 1850s, the concentration of them that existed in East Baltimore through the late nineteenth century marked the district off from the others as a particularly Jewish space. The recognition of the area as an ecclesiastical center was reinforced in 1876 when a new congregation, Chizuk Amuno, also built its synagogue on Lloyd Street, even though its members lived all over the city.[28] Moreover, among all of Baltimore's Jewish clusters, East Baltimore was the only one where Jews had moved precisely because they wanted to identify with Jewish institutions and partake in communal life. This factor further underscored the neighborhood's Jewish quality and contrasted it to the other hubs, which had attracted Jews with their markets and commercial strips.

Under the stewardship of Baltimore's Central European Jews, East Baltimore never became the kind of thickly Jewish enclave that later generations would come to know. Faced with a different sort of urban environment, a different set of economic circumstances, and a different context for acculturation and Americanization, the immigrants of the mid nineteenth century crafted a neighborhood that reflected their own particular social and cultural experience. While East Baltimore had few Jewish specialty stores, no sweatshops and no crowds of Yiddish-speaking immigrants during these years, it did attain a Jewish status that undoubtedly helped prepare the ground for the developments that were to follow in a very different time.

JEWISH EAST BALTIMORE CHANGES HANDS

Although fashionable areas on the west side of the city had been drawing upwardly mobile Central European Jews out of East Baltimore since the 1850s, the pace of outmigration began to accelerate toward the last quarter of the century. The move can be tracked best by the relocation of synagogues, keeping in mind that the congregations were following members who had already moved on to new locations.[29] As early as 1873, Har Sinai abandoned its High Street Temple for a new synagogue on Lexington Street, in the center of the thriving apparel district. Baltimore Hebrew Congregation, whose membership was larger, remained on Lloyd Street until 1889, leaving for a temporary location on Charles and Fayette Streets before moving in 1891 to a newly constructed edifice on Madison Street. According to a newspaper account, most members of the congregation, "which is a wealthy one," lived uptown and desired a more convenient—and presumably more prestigious—location for their place of worship.[30] Chizuk Amuno followed

in 1895 when it left Lloyd Street for new quarters on McCulloh and Mosher in Northwest Baltimore. Unlike its neighboring congregations, the Fells Point Hebrew Friendship Congregation never moved from Eden Street. As the exodus continued, it dwindled in membership, eventually passing out of existence in 1902.[31]

The movement out of East Baltimore was not a Jewish phenomenon alone, but part of a larger trend toward the end of the nineteenth century among middle- and upper-class residents who fled as Baltimore's center became increasingly industrialized, and the neighborhoods closest to downtown experienced an influx of working-class immigrants and African Americans. When the High Street Baptist Church sold its edifice after fifty years to move uptown, the *Baltimore Sun* reported that "the sale of the house of worship was determined upon because of its ineligible location," since "the neighborhood is fast becoming filled up with colored people and Polish Hebrews."[32] In addition to these groups, Italians, Greeks, Poles, and Lithuanians also became a significant presence in various parts of East Baltimore.[33]

Eastern European Jews became the dominant group in the area where the Central European Jews had once lived, having been attracted by the existing Jewish presence and the availability of synagogue buildings for their use.

The Concordia Association headquarters on German and Eutaw Streets, 1878.

Courtesy of the Enoch Pratt Free Library, Central Library/State Resource Center

Har Sinai Congregation occupied this building on West Lexington Street from 1873 to 1894. At the time of this photo, around 1910, the building housed the Ahavas Achim Congregation.

Jewish Museum of Maryland

Because the Jewish newcomers displaced not only their more Americanized coreligionists but also a large number of "old" immigrant groups and native-born Americans, most non-Jewish commentators could not help but see the transformation of the neighborhood as the hostile takeover of a respectable area. A writer for the *Sun* in 1895 wrote that once-stately homes of the English gentry still stood in Oldtown, but they now housed people and institutions foreign to their culture and sensibilities. The Carroll Mansion, located on East Lombard Street near Albemarle and home to one of Maryland's most prominent colonial families, was presented as a case in point. "Above its portal, instead of the coat of arms of the Carrolls," wrote the reporter, "is a Hebrew inscription telling that in the great salon there is now the synagogue of the 'People from Nieshin,' a town in Russia."[34] On another occasion, the same paper dubbed the Shot Tower, a city landmark built on East Fayette Street in 1828, "Baltimore's Tower of Babel" because of the polyglot "jargon"—meaning Yiddish—increasingly spoken in its environs.[35]

Although the influx of Eastern European Jews into East Baltimore was alarming to many native-born commentators, it did not occur overnight, but happened over several years, overlapping significantly with the ongoing departure of the Central European Jewish population. In the first years after their immigration to Baltimore, Jews from Poland and Russia avoided the East Baltimore neighborhood for the same reasons that Central Europeans had during their first years in the country. Mostly peddlers and retail merchants, they had to live in the areas that were most conducive to business. Thus, many settled in already established Jewish business areas like Harrison Street, where the first Eastern European synagogues were founded. In 1870, census records show that Harrison Street, along with Fells Point, had the two largest concentrations of Polish immigrants (undoubtedly Polish Jews) in the city.[36] By 1886, there was also a cluster of Polish Jews in the area around the Belair Market, where a large group leaving synagogue on Passover became embroiled in a street fight with an African American wagoneer who crashed into them.[37] Three years later, mention was made of Eastern European Jews living in Southwest Baltimore "in a colony on Pulaski street, near the car stables."[38]

The move of the initial wave of Polish and Russian Jews from areas such as Harrison Street into East Baltimore was a sign of upward mobility, as it had been for their Central European predecessors. Ultimately, however, as industrialization took hold and the immigrants increasingly found work in local sweatshops or in clothing factories in the manufacturing district, the neighborhood became a magnet for poorly paid Jews who wanted to be in Jewish surroundings and had no economic incentive to live in other parts of the city. Moreover, as the number of Eastern European Jews grew, they created an enclave large enough to support businesses whose Jewish owners preferred to remain among their countrymen. By the late 1880s and early 1890s, accounts began to identify East Baltimore as the chief gathering place of the new immigrants, even though they were still described as living

An early view of the Lombard Street market, 1880s.

Courtesy of the Ross J. Kelbaugh Collection, JMM 1988.226.5a.

throughout the city. "They are not contained to one locality, though a majority live downtown," reported the *Sun* in 1889. "Harrison, Low, South and North High and Exeter Streets, Lombard and Pratt and other streets in Oldtown contain these thrifty people." Two years later, the following description was given: "The Russian Jews in Baltimore are scattered through various parts of the city, but what is known as their colony is within the limits of from Front Street to Broadway and from Pratt to several squares beyond Baltimore Street."[39]

In the 1880s there was still a significant presence of Central European Jews in East Baltimore, although the community was clearly in transition. Based on the analysis of census records, the group seemed to be limited to three categories: those who continued to work in the Gay Street district and lived on the arteries that ran south from Gay Street to Fayette Street; Central European Jews who were poor, aged, or widowed and who, as a result, were not as economically or geographically mobile as the majority of their countrymen who were moving away; and more traditional Central European Jews for whom close proximity to a synagogue and other Jewish services was important.[40] This was especially true of leading members of Chizuk Amuno, like the Levys and some of the Friedenwalds, who were quite wealthy and prominent but retained their orthodox practices and affiliations.[41] This trend explains why Chizuk Amuno, a traditional congregation that broke away from Baltimore Hebrew in the 1870s, remained in the neighborhood as late as 1895, by which time the neighborhood had been thoroughly transformed into an enclave of Eastern European Jews.[42]

Chizuk Amuno's departure for uptown ended the presence of both Central European Jewish institutions and residents in East Baltimore, except for a small number of merchants who remained through World War I on North Gay Street, an area that had always retained a distinct character and was not considered part of the larger Jewish cluster to the south.[43] Meanwhile, during the first two decades of the twentieth century, a continual flow of new immigrants continued to arrive from Eastern Europe, helping to make East Baltimore into a more visibly Jewish part of the city, one crowded with synagogues, Hebrew schools, ethnic shopping areas, and Jewish institutions of all kinds. Like the German Jewish ghosts conjured by the young rabbi, Philip Graetz, few who had known Jewish East Baltimore in the 1850s and 1860s would have recognized it in the 1910s and 1920s.[44] Though built on the foundations of the earlier Jewish presence, it had now become a much different place, a reflection of both the changing times and its new inhabitants.

NOTES

1   Sidney L. Nyburg, *The Chosen People* (New York: Harper and Row, 1917), 193, 197-98.

2   This fact is well noted in the standard history of the Baltimore Jewish community, Isaac M. Fein's *The Making of an American Jewish Community: The History of Baltimore Jewry from 1773 to 1920* (Philadelphia: Jewish Publication Society of America, 1971), 77-78. Fein, however, exaggerates the importance of East Baltimore as the principal area for settlement for Central European Jews, who were far more spread out than he suggests.

3   These two were not the only Central European congregations later taken over by Eastern European Jewish immigrants. Congregation Aitz Chaim on Eden Street had formerly been home to the Fells Point Hebrew Friendship Congregation (Oheb Israel) and Congregation Anshe Sphard on High Street (later Congregation Anshe Bobruisk) was originally built as the High Street Temple of the Har Sinai Congregation. See Earl Pruce, *Synagogues, Temples and Congregations of Maryland, 1830-1890* (Baltimore: Jewish Historical Society of Maryland, 1993).

4   The term "Oldtown" dates to the eighteenth century and technically refers to the part of Baltimore originally incorporated as a separate entity called Jones Town. See J. Thomas Scharf, *History of Baltimore City and County* (Philadelphia: Louis H. Everts, 1881), 52-54. The southern boundary of Jones Town extended no further than the present-day Fayette Street, but during the nineteenth century, by which time the old boundaries had been forgotten by most Baltimoreans, Oldtown came to refer to a larger, less clearly defined area stretching down as far as East

Pratt Street. These were the rough boundaries of Oldtown employed in Fielding Lucas Jr.'s 1852 *Plan of the City of Baltimore,* and they will constitute the definition of Oldtown used in this essay. For similar usage, both in a period account and by a contemporary historian of the city, see *Baltimore Sun,* August 27, 1891, supplement, 4; and Sherry H. Olson, *Baltimore: The Building of an American City* (Baltimore: Johns Hopkins University Press, 1980), 229, 380.

5   I use here the translation preferred by the two historians of the congregation, Rabbi Adolph Guttmacher and Rose Greenberg. See Guttmacher, *A History of the Baltimore Hebrew Congregation, 1830-1905* (Baltimore: Lord Baltimore Press, 1905), 20; Greenberg, *Chronicle of Baltimore Hebrew Congregation, 1850-1975* (Baltimore: Baltimore Hebrew Congregation, 1976), 6. One might also render the name "the *dispersed* of Israel."

6   On the use of the name Nidche Yisrael by other congregations, see Jonathan D. Sarna, *American Judaism: A History* (New Haven: Yale University Press, 2004), 12; Sarna, "The Jews in British North America," in *The Jews and the Expansion of Europe to the West, 1450-1800,* ed. Paolo Bernardini and Norman Fiering (New York: Berghan Books, 2001), 520. On the self-styling of the founders of Baltimore Hebrew Congregation as the "scattered Israelites of Baltimore," see Greenberg, *Chronicle,* 5; Isidor Blum, *The Jews of Baltimore* (Baltimore: Historical Review Publishing Company, 1910), 7; and the original bill incorporating the congregation, in *Laws Made and Passed by the General Assembly of the State of Maryland* (Annapolis: Jeremiah Hughes, 1830), chap. 140.

7 Ira Rosenwaike, *On the Edge of Greatness: A Portrait of American Jewry in the Early National Period* (Cincinnati: American Jewish Archives, 1985), 51-52; Rosenwaike, "The Jews of Baltimore: 1820 to 1830," *American Jewish Historical Quarterly* 67 (September 1977): 260.

8 See Lance Sussman, "The Economic Life of the Jews in Baltimore as Reflected in the City Directories, 1819-1840," unpublished paper (1977), held by the American Jewish Archives, Cincinnati. Population figures are from Jacob Rader Marcus, *To Count a People: American Jewish Population Data, 1585-1984* (Lanham, Md.: University Press of America, 1990), 87; Rosenwaike, *On the Edge of Greatness*, 52.

9 Joseph Garonzik, "The Racial and Ethnic Make-up of Baltimore Neighborhoods, 1850-70," *Maryland Historical Magazine* 71 (Fall 1976): 397.

10 For the history of the area, see Norman G. Rukert, *The Fells Point Story* (Baltimore: Boche and Associates, 1976).

11 On the establishment of Baltimore's city markets, see Scharf, *History of Baltimore City and County*, 205-208. On market districts as a magnet for Jewish settlement during this period, see Joseph Hirschmann, "Housing Patterns of Baltimore Jews," *Generations* 2 (December 1981): 39-40. For a plotting of Baltimore Jewish residences and businesses as of 1840, see Sussman, "Economic Life of the Jews in Baltimore," 4-5.

12 Centre Market and Harrison Street can be glimpsed on the left side of the map on the inside front cover. For references to the street as a Jewish area during the nineteenth century, see *Baltimore Afro-American Ledger*, November 2, 1907, 4; and *Baltimore Jewish Times*, February 15, 1929, 18. Descriptions of Jewish businesses in these various hubs are based on a study of Baltimore city directories.

13 During the mid nineteenth century, all streets west of the Jones Falls were designated as "West." Charles Street became the dividing line between east and west—as it is today—in 1887, when all houses in Baltimore were renumbered. See *Baltimore Sun*, May 14, 1886, supplement, 2; and January 22, 1887, supplement, 2. For the quote on Baltimore Street and a general overview of business development in this area, see Edward K. Muller, "Spatial Order Before Industrialization: Baltimore's Central District, 1833-1860," in *Working Papers from the Regional Economic History Research Center* 4 (1981): 100-39, esp. 107.

14 On Central European Jews as peddlers in Maryland and neighboring states, see Eric L. Goldstein, "Beyond Lombard Street: Jewish Life in Maryland's Small Towns," in *We Call this Place Home: Jewish Life in Maryland's Small Towns*, ed. Karen Falk and Avi Y. Decter (Baltimore: Jewish Museum of Maryland, 2002), 27-79.

15 See Steven Lowenstein, *The Mechanics of Change: Essays in the Social History of German Jewry* (Atlanta: Scholars Press, 1992), 133-151.

16 On the European background of peddling and the forging of Jewish networks, see Hasia Diner, "Entering the Mainstream of Modern Jewish History: Peddlers and the American Jewish South," in *Jewish Roots in Southern Soil: A New History*, ed. Marcie Cohen Ferris and Mark I. Greenberg (Hanover, N.H.: University Press of New England, 2006), 90-92.

17 For these early synagogue locations, see Pruce, *Synagogues, Temples and Congregations*; and Blum, *The Jews of Baltimore*, 7.

18 See David Kaufman, *Cornerstones of Community: The Historic Synagogues of Maryland, 1845-1945* (Baltimore: Jewish Museum of Maryland), 17-22.

19 Meyer Hecht, biography of Samuel (Simeon) Hecht Jr., typescript, Jewish Museum of Maryland vertical files, 4.

20 Michael S. Franch, "The Congregational Community in the Changing City, 1840-1870," *Maryland Historical Magazine* 71 (Fall 1976): 372.

21 See both the residential and business entries for these men in the 1864 Baltimore City Directory, online at http://www.geocities.com/pauledely/1864/.

22 See, for example, the kosher butchers' ads in the *Jewish Chronicle* (Baltimore), January 1, 1875, 8; January 15, 1875, 7; and April 9, 1875, 8.

23 On the development of the area around Lexington and Howard Streets as a commercial district, see Dean Krimmel, "Merchant Princes and Their Palaces: The Emergence of Department Stores in Baltimore," in *Enterprising Emporiums: The Jewish Department Stores of Downtown Baltimore* (Baltimore: Jewish Museum of Maryland, 2001), 17, 20-21; and Muller, "Spatial Order Before Industrialization," 108. Interestingly, this cluster was also in the vicinity of a city market—the Lexington Market—although that seems to have been a less important factor in this case than in the creation of some of the other hubs.

24 Alexandra Lee Levin, *Vision: A Biography of Harry Friedenwald* (Philadelphia: Jewish Publication Society of America, 1964), 33.

25 *Baltimore Sun*, April 2, 1864, 2; September 5, 1864, 1. For descriptions of Purim balls and meetings of literary societies held in this neighborhood, see also *Baltimore Sun,* June 6, 1874, 2; April 7, 1875, 2; and June 7, 1875, 4.

26 On Shearith Israel and the other, more short-lived congregations on Howard Street, see Pruce, *Synagogues, Temples and Congregations*, 115-117, 118; and Dianne Feldman, "The Mystery of Rodeph Schalem," *Generations* (Fall 1998): 17-19.

27 Louis Cahn, *History of Oheb Shalom, 1853-1953* (Baltimore: Oheb Shalom Congregation, 1953), 19. On the continuing residential dispersion of Baltimore's Central European Jews in the mid to late nineteenth century, see Marsha L. Rozenblit, "Choosing a Synagogue: The Social Composition of Two German Congregations in Nineteenth-Century Baltimore," in *The American Synagogue: A Sanctuary Transformed*, ed. Jack Wertheimer (New York: Cambridge University Press, 1987), 330-332, 339. Rozenblit's references to East and West Baltimore are somewhat misleading, because she is unaware that the streets between Charles Street and the Jones Falls were not considered "East" before 1887. See footnote 13 above.

28 Jan Bernhardt Schein, *On Three Pillars: The History of Chizuk Amuno Congregation, 1871-1996* (Baltimore: Chizuk Amuno Congregation, 2000), 18.

29 On this general trend, see Rozenblit, "Choosing a Synagogue," 338-340, 352-354.

30 *Baltimore Sun*, February 4, 1889, 4.

31 Benjamin Friedman, "Synopsis of the History of the Baltimore-Fells Point Hebrew Friendship Congregation and its Cemetery and the Hebrew Friendship Cemetery Company," typescript, 1910, vertical file, Jewish Museum of Maryland (filed under "Hebrew Friendship Congregation"), 4.

32 *Baltimore Sun,* October 10, 1890, 4.

33 See Gilbert Sandler, *The Neighborhood: The Story of Baltimore's Little Italy* (Baltimore: Bodine and Associates, 1974), 23-25; D. Randall Beirne, "The Impact of Black Labor on European Immigration into Baltimore's Oldtown, 1790-1910," *Maryland Historical Magazine* 83 (Winter 1988): 338-343. Baltimore Hebrew Congregation was sold to a congregation of Lithuanian Catholics. See *Baltimore Sun*, February 4, 1889, 4.

34 *Baltimore Sun,* August 24, 1895, 10.

35 *Baltimore Sun*, December 16, 1893, 8.

36 Garonzik, "Racial and Ethnic Make-up," 396.

37 *Baltimore Sun,* April 28, 1886, 4.

38 *Baltimore Sun,* January 2, 1889, supplement, 1.

39 Ibid.; *Baltimore Sun,* August 27, 1891, supplement, 4.

40 Based on a study of U.S. Census Schedules for Baltimore City, 1880.

41 On the traditionalism of the Friedenwalds, see Levin, *Vision*, 34, 39, 54-55, 76. On the Levy family, see Jessica Elfenbein, "Uptown and Traditional," *Southern Jewish History* 9 (2006): 69-102.

42 On Chizuk Amuno, see Schein, *On Three Pillars*; Nancy J. Ordway, "A History of Chizuk Amuno Congregation: An American Synagogue" (Ph.D. dissertation, Baltimore Hebrew University, 1997); and Rozenblit, "Choosing a Synagogue," 343-52.

43 On the Central European Jews who remained on Gay Street, see Philip Kahn, Jr., *Uncommon Threads: Threads That Wove the Fabric of Baltimore's Jewish Life* (Baltimore: Pecan Publications, 1996), 48-49.

44 On this point, see Michael Aaronsohn, *Broken Lights* (Cincinnati: Johnson and Hardin Co., 1946), 39.

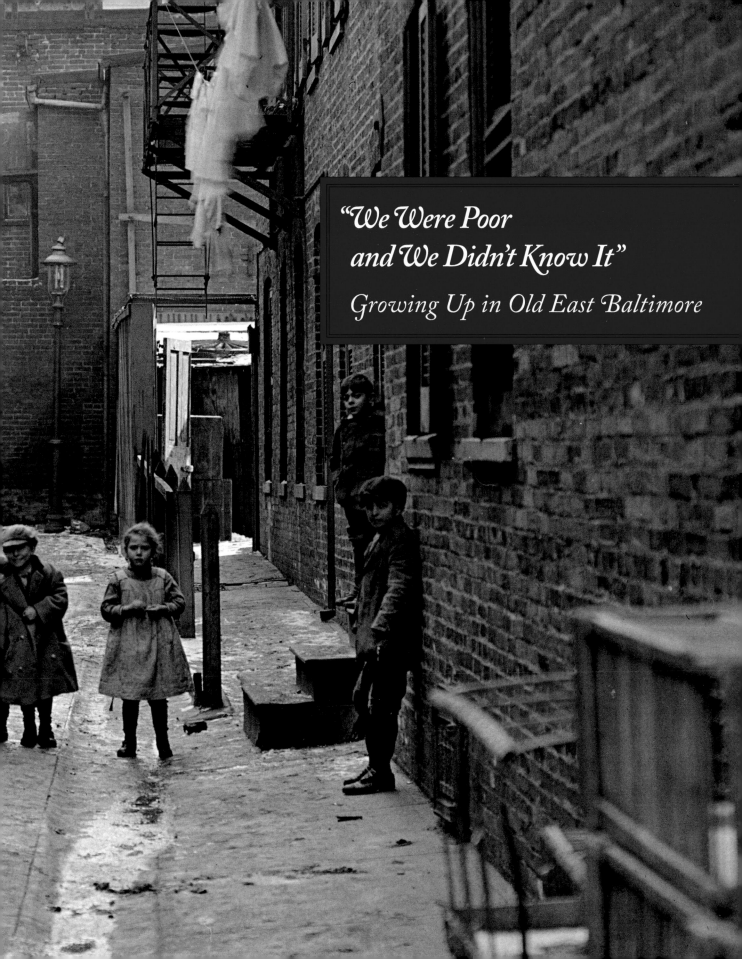

"We Were Poor and We Didn't Know It"

Growing Up in Old East Baltimore

"We Were Poor and We Didn't Know It": Growing Up in Old East Baltimore

BY ANITA KASSOF

Anita Kassof is Associate Director of the Jewish Museum of Maryland.

OVERLEAF: *Children at play in an alley near Fayette Street, circa 1905.*

Courtesy of The Maryland Historical Society

Rena Kolman, who grew up in East Baltimore in the 1920s and 1930s, fondly remembers evenings spent in the tiny grocery store that belonged to a friend's mother. When the shop—carved from a rowhouse front room—closed at the end of each day, Kolman and her neighbors gathered there to sing and play the harmonica. "We didn't have to spend money to have fun. We had a lot of fun doing whatever came naturally," she recalls, describing the big breadboxes that doubled as benches and the easy camaraderie the evenings engendered.[1]

Memoirs and oral histories of people who grew up in the Jewish immigrant enclave of East Baltimore in the first half of the twentieth century paint a picture of a tightly knit community where shared circumstances blunted the worst indignities of poverty. Everything—from schools and recreation centers to shops and synagogues—was within easy reach. Traditional Judaism and deeply internalized customs provided a safe and comfortable berth, and the possibilities offered by a growing economy held promise that East Baltimore's children would do better than their parents, despite many hardships.

From the vantage point of five or more decades later, these narrators describe happy childhoods. Although many families lived at the margins, where missing a single week's pay could mean eviction or destitution, former residents describe not the daily privations, but the plenty of their mother's kitchens, the excitement of chasing the ice truck on hot summer days, and the delight of winning a basketball game at the Jewish Educational Alliance. In his memoir, Louis Shecter asks, "What about the stories of dirt, poverty, ignorance, even repulsive people? Obviously those things must have been there. However . . . the unpleasant facts did not stay with me."[2]

Upbeat childhood memories obscure the fact that for this transitional generation, caught between the old world represented by their parents and the new world promised by America, life was tough. Fathers seemed always to be at work, while mothers simultaneously tended to family businesses and ran the household. Housewives walked blocks to save a penny on a loaf of bread, spent hours plucking fowl to fill comforters, and fashioned pillowcases out of old flour sacks. A new pair of shoes—purchased once a year before the High Holidays—was a thing to behold, and most people took their weekly showers at the public baths because their own small apartments lacked hot running water. The streets were crowded, the living quarters cramped, and the stench of privies and livestock filled the air. Though former residents of East Baltimore might laughingly recall sneaking to the outhouse at night, candle in hand, to read novels, urban reformers described those same facilities as "indescribably foul." And social workers warned that the neighborhood's unwholesome atmosphere was a breeding ground for juvenile delinquency.[3]

The very qualities that reformers sought to eradicate—dense settlement, narrow alleys, and mixed-use areas—delighted generations of immigrant children. Streets were overcrowded, but neighbors knew one another and

responsible adult eyes were often on the children—"sort of like family," as one former resident recalled. A mixed-use neighborhood that encompassed stores, synagogues, schools, recreation halls, workplaces, and apartments might not have lived up to the nascent suburban ideal of separate spheres for home and work, but it meant that children could be independent because everything they needed was within walking distance. And although the immigrants might have seemed dark and foreign to native observers, the old world group provided a safe and familiar community for East Baltimore's children.[4]

More than anything else, East Baltimore invited its children to interact directly with life in all of its grimy, gritty wonder. In the process, they enjoyed themselves mightily. The neighborhood offered a universe of possibilities. The rain-gorged Jones Falls became a roaring river that drew young anglers wielding makeshift nets, hoping to catch stray balls floating downstream from neighborhoods in north Baltimore. The junk heap behind a novelty store offered the raw material for homemade toys. The brothels that lined Watson Street and the pool halls and peep shows of Baltimore Street offered a glimpse of the seamier side of urban living, a reality that even the most conscientious mother could not conceal from her curious offspring.

If the written record indicates poverty, overcrowding, and crime, why are former residents' memories, by and large, so positive? The contrasts between dire contemporaneous reports and glowing recollections would seem to discount the validity of oral recollections, were it not for the fact that narrator

TOP: *Rena Kolman and friends outside her family's home on Fairmount Avenue, June 1924.*

Courtesy of Rena Kolman, JMM L2006.19.4

BOTTOM: *Dave Spigel and Alvin "Bommie" Lazen clown around in East Baltimore, circa 1940.*

Courtesy of Jerome Sefret, JMM L2007.6.2.12

The courtyard of an East Baltimore tenement, circa 1907. The image appeared in a report decrying the terrible conditions in the neighborhood.

Courtesy of the Wisconsin Historical Society

after narrator echoes a similar sentiment, summed up by Kathryn Rodbell Sollins, daughter of an immigrant baker: "I didn't know that I was poor. 'Course I was happy, I had my parents, I was never hungry, I never wanted for everything because what I needed was there. My needs were small. Those . . . were good years."[5]

Taken together, oral and written accounts present a more nuanced picture than either alone could. Filtered through the prism of time, descriptions of the past tend to minimize bad experiences and focus on good, but that does not mean they are false. Memories of old East Baltimore, like many people's reflections about childhood, have been polished by time and enriched by the realization that they reflect a disappeared place and a vanished way of life. It is hardly surprising that this fleeting moment in the history of Baltimore Jewry—when immigrant culture flourished and the newcomers had yet to abandon the crowded streets of the old neighborhood for the leafy suburbs of Northwest Baltimore—evokes such profound longing. Not only have the physical structures that lent shape to so many childhoods been demolished, a way of life in which work, family, home, and community shared a single sphere, has disappeared.

PARENTS AND CHILDREN

The immigrants' purpose was to open up the world to their children.

Joseph Hirschmann

Relations between parents and children were shaped by the conditions of the East Baltimore immigrant neighborhood, which was in a state of flux in the first half of the twentieth century. From the 1890s to the start of World War I in 1914, a steady flow of Eastern European Jews arrived in Baltimore, and most of them settled in an area roughly bounded by the Jones Falls to the west, Caroline Street to the east, Pratt Street to the south, and Fayette Street to the north (see map, inside front cover). Although immigrants tended to move out of the enclave as they acclimated and prospered, others arrived constantly to replace them.

Avrum Rifman, who grew up on South Caroline Street in the 1910s, remembers that his mother regularly welcomed new arrivals from the old country. "Until they got started, they had free board and lodging. Because of the limited number of beds available, some of the immigrants literally slept on the boards of the large kitchen floor, using a heavy blanket for a mattress, and a sheet with an overcoat on top of it to ward off the cold of the night. The women got jobs in the shirt factories. The men, who had no special skills, were introduced to 'arabbing' [peddling] until they saved enough money to buy a small candy store or grocery store, open seven days a week and seven nights a week." Harry Attman, who went on to found a delicatessen dynasty, came to Baltimore because he had friends who were already established here. He, in turn, welcomed relatives when they arrived from Europe in the 1920s.[6]

The newcomers kept East Baltimore vibrant and assured that it retained its Jewish flavor. By infusing the neighborhood with a dose of the old world, their presence moderated Americanizing forces and slowed the assimilation of those who came before. As long as Jews could live in a cohesive immigrant neighborhood, there was less urgency to adapt to American ways. Many elderly residents never bothered to learn English. There was no need, when neighbors and shopkeepers alike conversed in Yiddish.

World War I temporarily halted the influx of immigrants, and federal legislation brought it to a near standstill in the early 1920s. The immigrant enclave declined in the twenties and thirties, as Jewish residents moved steadily east toward Patterson Park or northwest to neighborhoods around Druid Hill Park. While around 70 percent of the neighborhood's households

Solomon and Fannie Rodbell with their children, David, Dora, Isidore, Kathryn, and Jacob, 1905.

Gift of Leonard Sollins, JMM 1995.160.1

45

Chaim and Zeesla Baile Rifman with their children, Avrum and Ruchel, circa 1907.

Jewish Museum of Maryland

were Jewish in 1900, the percentage dropped to around 60 percent in 1920, and 45 percent in 1930. As Jews moved out, they were replaced mostly by Italians and African Americans. [7]

Throughout this period, a gulf separated American-born children from their immigrant parents. Unlike their elders, they had no experience of life in Europe. Daily, they were exposed to things at school and on the street that their parents could not understand. And while their elders' first language was Yiddish, the children of immigrants conversed in English. Paul Wartzman remembers that at home, his parents spoke Yiddish, Polish, and "broken English." Hymen Saye commented, "We never spoke a word of English to [our parents]. We spoke English among ourselves but when we came home, we dropped English at the doorstep because my parents never made an effort to learn English."[8] Children often served as translators and intermediaries, parenting their parents as they acclimated to life in unfamiliar territory.

Immigrant Jewish families came under assault from all sides. External forces, such as the street, the schools, and the movie houses, threatened their cohesion. Division came from within, too, as children struggled to dissociate themselves from their parents' old-world ways in order to become fully American. Eric Pernikoff, who grew up in the 1930s, remembers that "the children really didn't follow their parents because they thought they were too old fashioned."[9]

Children regarded their parents with a mixture of gratitude and shame. While most were well aware of the sacrifices their mothers and fathers made on their behalf—including leaving a familiar homeland in search of a more secure future—they also experienced feelings of impatience and embarrassment about their "greenhorn" parents. For most children of immigrants, being American was effortless. Just as their parents struggled to comprehend American life and assimilate modern customs, their children had only a second-hand understanding of what it meant to be dislocated and to start over again, gleaned from watching their parents' struggles. Lack of understanding distanced parents and children. As one contemporary observer wrote of the immigrant experience on New York's Lower East Side, the child's "talent for caricature is developed often at the expense of his parents, his race, and all 'foreigners'; for he is an American, he is 'the people,' and like his glorious countrymen in general, he is quick to ridicule the stranger. He laughs at the foreign Jew with as much heartiness as at the 'dago'; for he feels that he himself is almost as remote from the one as from the other."[10]

In order to be truly American, some children willfully broadened the emotional and cultural gulf that already separated them from their parents. Their parents' reticence about life in Europe made that easier. Most parents rarely, if ever, spoke about life in Europe or arrival in America, as if ignoring their roots could erase them. Reflection about one's past—especially a past that was both literally and figuratively "foreign"—is, to a certain degree, a luxury reserved for people who have distanced themselves from it by rein-

George Boltansky with his daughter Shirley in the family's store at 1150 East Lombard Street, circa 1942.

Gift of Samuel Boltansky, JMM 1990.96.1a

venting themselves. Perhaps sensing that the upheavals and uncertainties that accompanied immigration diminished their authority over their families, parents were not eager to remind their children where they came from. And for children hungry to make their mark on America, the past was an unnecessary distraction from their hopeful strivings.

CHILDREN AT WORK

I used to go down to my father's store and I used to work, every day right after school.
Edward Attman

The case of the Goldsmith family of 919 East Baltimore Street provides a vivid example of the perils that could befall a family as immigrant parents struggled to gain a foothold. A report prepared by caseworkers for the Hebrew Benevolent Society recounted the family's turbulent existence over the course of more than a decade. It opened with a 1910 notation that Mrs. Goldsmith had been confined to Johns Hopkins Hospital, leaving her five sons, ages four to eleven, in the care of a neighbor. It noted that the family had run out of coal and exhausted its credit with the local butcher, and that the house was filthy. In 1912, the caseworker reported that Joe, the Goldsmith's eldest son, had dropped out of school to go to work. Over the next several years, the Benevolent Society tried valiantly to keep the three oldest Goldsmith sons—Joe, Abe, and Nathan—in school. Ultimately, their efforts failed.[11]

The Goldsmith history is an extreme case of the travails resulting from

The Saye family (left to right), Fanny, Hymen, Ida, Louis, Sara, and Bertha, circa 1910.

Gift of Hymen Saye, JMM 1991.7.5

children's involvement in the family economy. Even better-established families, though, were likely to call on their children to work. They sold newspapers, worked in sweatshops, or ran deliveries and worked behind the counter in the family store. Milton Schwartz's relatives owned Crystal's Bakery, a neighborhood landmark. He remembers, "My uncle would sit me on the counter sometimes, a little kid, and I used to fill the donuts with the cream, or éclairs, I'd get a big kick out of that."[12]

Other children were forced to step in when they lost a parent. At three, Morris Gordon lost his father to influenza. By eight, he was selling newspapers on the street corner and giving his wages to his mother. His modest earnings were vital to the family's well-being and he handed them over without resentment. Kathryn Rodbell Sollins was born in 1901, seven years after her parents immigrated to the United States. Her father scrimped, saved, and finally managed to purchase his own bakery. Although she was expected to work in the family business—delivering loaves of bread each morning—Kathryn attended school once her chores were done. But then her father contracted tuberculosis, possibly from breathing in the dusty flour day after day. He died prematurely, leaving a widow and five children. At twelve years of age, Kathryn left school and found work as a stock girl to help support the family.[13]

Likewise, Bertha Saye was forced to leave school to contribute to the family's upkeep, even though her younger brother, Hymen, had the opportunity to complete his education and realize his dream of becoming a teacher. Hymen recalls that it was "accepted fact that the parents set a goal for their children to do better than what the parents had done. The parents were the first generation, they did not want their children to be needle workers or pushcart drivers or work in the Belair Market. They wanted their children to be somebody and get ahead."[14]

Hymen had two distinct advantages over his sister: he was younger, and he was male. Generally, girls were more likely than boys to interrupt their educations prematurely. Many parents, exhausted from working to keep their families afloat, had little energy to spare for childrearing. Big sisters often raised their younger siblings. It was not uncommon to see a group of preadolescent girls at play on the sidewalk, a passel of toddlers in tow. Birth order also determined how long an immigrant child was likely to stay in school, with older children more likely than their younger brothers and sisters to leave.[15]

Some managed to stay in school because their parents refused to give up on their futures regardless of the personal toll. Charles Solomon's father often put in eighteen hour days in his tailor shop, but he never asked for his children's help there. "I didn't have any chores," recalls the younger Solomon. "My father always used to tell me to pay attention to my school work. He didn't want me to become interested in tailoring because he used to say that he wanted me to amount to something."[16]

East Baltimore's public schools were powerful agents of Americanization and assimilation. Henry Burke recalls that his parents named him Gershon but, since he had a number of relatives with the same name, they called him Harry. When his teacher called roll on the first day of school, however, she told him that Harry was only a nickname. Then and there, she dubbed him Henry, a "proper" name for an American boy. Education widened the gap between parents and children, providing youngsters with a distinctly American frame of reference. A 1924 *Baltimore Sun* article about East Baltimore Jewish life commented, "There is one subject upon which the younger generation is in harmony with those that went before it. Nowhere does one find girls or boys more appreciative of the educational advantages of the new land. . . . There is Bernard Siegel, in knickers and cap, who will . . . expatiate upon the advantages of the Junior High School at which he is a student. This youth's parents are by no means fluent in their use of English; the English of the son is both fluent and correct."[17]

As public schools weaned them from their parents' influence, children found themselves caught between two worlds. By the time they reached junior high school, many had attained more education than their parents. Overwhelmed and intimidated, some immigrant parents simply withdrew. Paul Goodman explains that his parents were "old timers." He continues: "My mother or father never ever went to see me in school, to meet my teacher, to see how I was doing or anything like that. My father was too busy, he worked from morning 'til night . . . and my mother didn't speak English, so between the two of them they said, 'I'm sure you're doing okay.'"[18]

The Streets of East Baltimore

My world consisted of a neighborhood bounded by Central Avenue and Exeter Street. That was my shtetl.
Perry Siegel

Many people who grew up in East Baltimore comment that "everybody knew everybody else" and a large number use the term "we" when recalling their childhoods, suggesting that neighbors shared both experiences and aspirations. Together with a cohort of other young Jewish scholars, Hymen Saye pursued a rigorous course of study, attending City College High School at the same time that he studied Jewish education at Baltimore Hebrew College. "All of these things took time and we were young and our bodies could take it, so we didn't sleep very long. We got home at midnight and the next morning we had to be back at City College once again. And we didn't drive to City College, we walked. Ten cents was very hard to come by." This sense of community and common mission made hard work seem less arduous. As Aaron Smelkinson recalls, "Nobody showed off or felt superior to the next one. Everyone got along very, very nicely." Certainly, Smelkinson's recollections have been burnished by time. Nonetheless, the positive slant of shared memories suggests that although East Baltimore's residents were poor, they were far from impoverished culturally, socially, and spiritually. A sense of shared circumstances, a supportive community of people from similar backgrounds, and a network of adults who expected their children and their neighbors' children to take advantage of the opportunities America offered made for childhoods that were rich in possibility and hope.[19]

The close proximity of home, work, recreation, and worship also tended to bring people together. Gail Davis recalls that East Baltimore offered a "very concentrated way to live." Within a radius of several blocks, children were educated and entertained, attended synagogue, participated in community meetings or took in performances at the Yiddish theater, and stirred up excitement on the streets that were their playground. A 1929 report from the Associated Jewish Charities extolled the virtues of this tightly settled area: "East Baltimore is a little city in itself. It can be said that an individual dwelling in this section could live a full normal life without depending on any of the other sections of the city for his needs. The industrial, recreational, educational, health, cultural, housing, and shopping advantages which East Baltimore offers cannot be overestimated."[20]

Nowhere was the neighborhood's mixed-use character more apparent

50

Hymen Saye teaching at the Baltimore Talmud Torah, 1928.

Gift of Jerry Cohen for Hymen Saye, JMM 1991.7.15

than on Lombard Street, the neighborhood's busy commercial marketplace. Jerome Sefret recalls that it seemed to him that "everyone's" parents worked on Lombard Street and lived above their stores. His recollections are not too far from reality. The 1930 City Directory lists fifty-eight businesses (fifty-two Jewish- and six Italian-owned) in the two block stretch of Lombard Street that was the heart of the Jewish marketplace, and in most cases shop owners' home and work addresses were the same.[21]

Merchants' wares spilled from their storefronts onto the sidewalks, mingling with the goods offered by pushcart peddlers. Housewives haggled for bargains, delivery trucks and wagons clattered by on the cobblestones, and everywhere there were children. Much of life was lived on the streets. Apartments were small, and often a single room served as kitchen, living room, parlor and—when a galvanized tub was pulled out on Fridays—bathroom as well. It is no wonder, then, that children longed for the openness and freedom that the streets and sidewalks offered. This was their territory, a place beyond their parents' gaze, where they pried loose cobblestones for ammunition in street battles, played marbles or potsy (hopscotch), and

TOP: *Children at play on the corner of Pratt and Albemarle Streets, 1907.*

Courtesy of the R.L. Harris collection, Flag House and Star-Spangled Banner Museum

BOTTOM: *Lombard Street, 1927.*

Gift of Earl Pruce, JMM 1985.90.8

Children at play in City Springs Park, 1914. Located along Lombard Street between Eden and Spring Streets, the park was a favorite destination for East Baltimore's children.

Courtesy of The Maryland Historical Society

ran barefoot in the summertime. In a 1988 reminiscence, Al Olschansky writes, "I was seven years old, and, being the eldest of four children, I was allowed to roam the streets at will after school hours." One can imagine that Olschansky's mother, at home in a cramped apartment with his three younger siblings, was only too glad to see him go. [22]

Although the streets offered liberation, children were keenly aware that "their" territory was strictly circumscribed. As long as they were on their own turf, Jewish children were ascendant. But their sense of familiarity and comfort quickly disappeared if they wandered into alien territory. Venturing east toward Patterson Park, they might be taunted with cries of "Christ Killer" or "Dirty Jew." In the Italian neighborhood to the south, sweet, syrupy frozen snowballs could be had for a bargain, but the intrepid boy who headed there to save a penny might suddenly find himself surrounded by a hostile gang.

Sometimes trouble came looking for children on their own terrain. Paul Wartzman describes walking home from the Jewish Educational Alliance after an evening's recreation: "I was short and fat and I had a little something I was putting my clothes into, a duffle bag. And out of Exeter and Lombard Street there comes this group of Italian guys, and the one guy was tall. He wasn't a bad guy, but he was mischievous. And he came up to me and he said, 'Hey, Jew,' he said, 'I want you to get me some stuff out of your bakery.'"

Petrified, Wartzman unlocked his father's bakery and gave the boy some buns. Years later, he laughingly recalls, his tormenter became a city councilman, and Wartzman presented him with a congratulatory bag of buns.[23]

Aggression cut both ways; Jewish children could be perpetrators as well as victims. Gang rivalry was, to some, simply part of growing up. Isadore Livov recalls: "Now, during youth, what do young boys have to do? They like to fight, right? We used to pick battles with the *schwarzes* (blacks) who lived on Fairmount Avenue. We used to have gangs. . . . The white gangs would hide behind the wall and we would have teasers to get the *schwarzes* to run by, so we could waylay them. We used to specialize in battles." Yet, in the same oral history, Livov reminisces about his friendship with a black boy named Jimmy Brown, describing how they played together outdoors. The two remained friends until they entered school—Livov the all-white P.S. 93 and Brown a nearby "colored" school—and institutionalized segregation drove them apart.[24]

Although name calling, petty extortion, and exclusion certainly stung, some recall that ethnic conflict in the neighborhood was essentially harmless. As Seymour Attman put it, "It was child's play. It was always Jews against the gentiles but I wouldn't say it was as antisemitic as some things are today, because after all you lived in the neighborhood, you worked in the neighborhood and everybody tried to help one another out."[25]

Living in poverty, children were forced to be resourceful. Pocket change was a rare treat, to be jealously hoarded and then carefully spent on a slice of watermelon, a handful of penny candy, or "calcamanias," temporary tattoos that were all the rage among East Baltimore's younger set. Children made their own toys, fashioning carts out of baskets and stray wheels. Even small children found simple entertainment on the streets. Isadore Livov remembers that as a young boy he enjoyed walking by Miller's Dairy, where he watched in rapt fascination as a worker sterilized milk cans with a big hose. Meanwhile, his sister Norma spent hours playing on the granite steps of a local synagogue.[26]

The neighborhood's stores were the source of both everyday necessities and a wondrous array of tempting novelties. Children could wile away an afternoon at Klein's toy store on the corner of Pratt and High Streets, which always stocked the latest gadgets. "Anything new that would come out for children [Mr. Klein] would have," says Charles Solomon. "He had an 'electric' machine too. You would hold a knob and he would hold another knob. Then Mr. Klein would increase the charge gradually and the kids competed to see how much of a charge they could stand. This was a test of their strength." On Baltimore Street, Hendler's Creamery was a beloved neighborhood institution. If a child gathered enough courage to enter its main office, he would be rewarded with a paper cup of fresh ice cream.[27]

Jewish-owned businesses and Jewish residents seemed, from the perspective of a youngster, to be everywhere. "It was strictly Jewish," says Joe Mandell, "the undertaker across the street, the little Jewish Turkish bath, Jewish tailors,

Alvin "Bommie" Lazen, Jerome Sefret, and Ely Attman in front of Atlantic Imports, 1119 East Lombard Street.

Courtesy of Jerome Sefret, JMM L2007.6.2.7

53

Hendler's Creamery, 1100 East Baltimore Street.

Gift of James M. Haney, JMM 1997.16.1

Jewish doctors. . . ." On Saturday the stores were shuttered, the air was thick with the comforting scent of cholent, the thick stew that Jewish house-wives made for the Sabbath, and everyone in the neighborhood seemed to be headed for synagogue. In an atmosphere suffused with *Yiddishkeit*, being Jewish came as naturally as breathing. Some youngsters crossed ethnic and racial barriers to befriend non-Jewish and even African American children, but the majority socialized with other Jewish youths. A Jewish child could go into his friend's house, comfortable in the assurance that he would be offered familiar, kosher foods.[28]

Although Jews shared the streets with African Americans, Italians, and other non-Jewish immigrants, the neighborhood had an overwhelmingly Jewish flavor, expressed in the variety of Jewish foods in its stores, the syna-gogues that dotted nearly every block, and the sound of Yiddish heard on the streets. Most children—boys and girls—attended one of the many afternoon Hebrew schools, and some boys received extra tutoring from local scholars. One tutor, Reb Bennett, left a strong impression on his former students. Since he did double duty as a *schochet* (kosher slaughterer), he routinely came to class with blood caked under his fingernails and splattered on his apron.[29]

Deeply ingrained traditions carried across the Atlantic informed the everyday behavior of the immigrants. They continued to look to their local rabbis for guidance in spiritual and practical matters. Women cooked the way their mothers and grandmothers before them had—turning out sweet poppy seed cakes and savory chicken soup—and treated their children with familiar folk remedies. In an unpublished memoir, Avrum Rifman writes about surviving a bout of typhoid fever: "I remember that for two days and nights, Mrs. S. standing alongside of my mother, both cracking ice with their teeth and making me swallow broken pieces of the soothing ice until I fell into a deep slumber. In the afternoon of the second day, I opened my eyes and I heard Mrs. S. and my mother whispering to each other, '*Gott zu danken, ehr gait leben*' (Thanks to God, he will live)."[30]

Going to synagogue was a routine occurrence rather than an occasion reserved for Rosh Hashanah and Yom Kippur. Since the synagogue was very much a part of everyday life, it was not unusual for young boys—dressed in their holiday best—to escape its familiar confines even on the highest Holy Days to squeeze in a game of nuts on the sidewalk. Kneeling on the pave-ment, they carefully arranged hazelnuts into pyramids to see whether their opponents could knock them down. Spinning nuts was a holiday tradition and the boys played with an obsessive passion. Paul Wartzman recalls the Passover when his friend had his foot run over by a delivery truck as he was spinning nuts. "Harold was at the hospital but we kept playing nuts," he chuckles. The game carried other hazards, as well. "You only got clothes on Pesach and Rosh Hashanah, a new pair of pants and shoes," remembers Milton Schwartz. "And I came home with a hole in my pants, on my knee, from playing nuts all day long. I thought my mother was gonna put a hole in my head!"[31]

54

Paul Wartzman (right) with his brother Sam and his nephew Leigh Naftolin, circa 1939.

Courtesy of Paul Wartzman, JMM CP19.2007.1

RECREATION AND REFORM

The Jewish Educational Alliance was a wonderful organization. It took young people off the street.

Isadore Livov

East Baltimore's streets may have served as playgrounds, but they also harbored both naked and concealed dangers. Crowding bred filth and disease. Before Baltimore established a sanitary sewer system in the 1910s, backyard privies often overflowed, spewing their stinking contents into the muddy yards and alleyways. Nostalgic recollections of old East Baltimore often invoke the Lombard Street chicken slaughterers who served up fresh poultry to order. But they usually overlook the fact that the chickens' blood ran in the gutters, that flies and feathers were "everywhere," and that "in hot weather the smell from such yards [was] sickening." A 1913 report cited, among East Baltimore's hazards, "bawdy houses, all night poolrooms, low dance halls, debasing movie shows, and the hotels which harbor the floating and transient vice of other cities."[32]

The rooftop playground at the Jewish Educational Alliance.

Gift of Jack Chandler, JMM 1991.231.29

A double outhouse in East Baltimore, 1907.

Courtesy of The Maryland Historical Society

OPPOSITE TOP: *A Jewish Educational Alliance basketball team.*

Gift of Jack Chandler, JMM 1992.231.14

OPPOSITE BOTTOM: *Needlepoint at the Jewish Educational Alliance "Home Camp" at 1216 East Baltimore Street, 1947.*

JMM 1999.88.2

Shared traditions and a sense that everyone in the neighborhood knew everyone else could only go so far in protecting and nurturing children. Social workers and progressive reformers identified East Baltimore's crowded streets and disreputable establishments as breeding grounds for delinquency. "Keeping children off the street" became the code phrase for preserving the young from corruption, and for molding them into upright Americans. In immigrant neighborhoods throughout the country, settlement houses sprang up, offering wholesome recreation for children and a menu of enriching and educational activities for their parents. Between 1913 and 1952 the Jewish Educational Alliance at 1216 East Baltimore Street served thousands of children, providing a lifeline for many who might otherwise have succumbed to the lure of the streets. "God knows what jails we'd be in now if it wasn't for the JEA," recalled one grateful former patron in a 1980 article in the *Baltimore Sun*.[33]

A listing of activities that ran nearly half a page in the October 1930 issue of the *Baltimore Jewish Times* shows a typical JEA schedule. For children there were sports, crafts, dancing, drama, and foreign language instruction. Boys competed in athletic leagues and joined the debating club, played caroms in the game room and learned woodworking. Isadore Livov still treasures the footstool, hand mirror, nut bowl, and carved wooden chest he made in the JEA's woodworking shop. For girls, there were classes in sewing and embroidery, needlework, painting, dressmaking, rug hooking, and home economics. Their parents might enroll in an "educational series" that included sessions on the "Aesthetics of Dress," "Personal Hygiene," "Interior Decorating and Furnishing of Small Apartments," and the "Aesthetics of Behavior." The JEA also offered a free day nursery for preschoolers whose parents worked or who could not take care of them "because of a domestic difficulty at home."[34]

Such offerings blurred the boundaries between recreation and reform. As the JEA taught East Baltimore's children how to play piano or build model airplanes, it also imparted lessons about cooperation, constructive competition, and healthy debate—all values associated with the American democratic system. "We really became people [at the JEA]," says Paul Wartzman. "That's where I learned how to speak and that's where I learned how to get along with people and that's where I learned how to associate in organizations." The JEA's influence extended beyond its walls and into the community. In a 1920 report, the JEA's resident director described the disruptive "flood" of children who came to the JEA in the evening. In response, he wrote, his staff had "begun visiting the various mothers and have asked for their promise to put the children to bed at 8 o'clock," a bedtime he judged much more wholesome. Jerome Sefret recalls the time JEA director Nathan Berlin visited his family's house to invite him to form a club with his peers. Sefret dutifully complied, rounding up his playmates and establishing the JEA's Titan Club with about twenty other neighborhood boys.[35]

JEA staff members approached their commitment to "bettering" the chil-

A dance class at the Jewish Educational Alliance, 1937.

Gift of Jack Chandler, JMM 1992.231.79

dren of East Baltimore with a crusading spirit: "I have never known how hard it was to be cheerful and patient until now when I see how our new workers are sorely tried by the Jewish aggressiveness of our boys and girls," wrote the resident director in 1921. "Yet they are doing very well and are entering into our esprit de corps." In occasionally overblown language, staff reports warned of pool parlors and gambling dens, drug stores that distributed narcotics, and all-too-attractive burlesque houses. Staff saw the JEA as a "stalwart warrior" engaged in battle against such evil institutions. In a particularly vivid 1921 report, an unidentified staff member declared that the JEA must "use every weapon in its warfare against undesirable influences, resulting from commercialized and unsupervised amusements. It also must place upon its shoulders the tremendous burden of providing supervised educational and recreational opportunities—more attractive than outside diversions."[36]

In large measure, the JEA succeeded. In terms of sheer numbers alone, it was a formidable community influence; another 1921 report estimated that on average, 18,000 people, mostly children, used the JEA each month.[37] Although the JEA closed its Baltimore Street building in 1952, today its alumni membership remains 400-strong and reunions draw several hundred participants each year. Their commitment to their shared past attests to the strength of the bonds formed at the Alliance, and points up the difference between lived history and the perspective of outsiders who chronicled it. While reformers saw in the JEA a vehicle for improving and teaching a generation of new Americans, East Baltimore's children simply had a good time in the beloved building where they made lifelong friendships.

A Vanishing Way of Life

We were like such a dying breed, you know, we last few children of East Baltimore. We were the last children of the old world.   Gail Davis

To those Jewish children who remained in East Baltimore into the 1940s, the neighborhood sometimes felt like a ghost town. Although Jewish-owned businesses continued to thrive on Lombard Street, East Baltimore was no longer the bustling Jewish residential community it had once been. Norma Wolod remembers that when she was a teenager in the late 1930s, the neighborhood changed completely. "I had no friends, nobody, in the area." In the new lexicon of urban reformers, East Baltimore was a "blighted slum area." City officials cited East Baltimore's substandard housing as a source of juvenile delinquency and disease, and targeted it for demolition as "bankrupt." Such areas "are like festering sores," one report read, "spreading their contagion." [38]

East Baltimore's upwardly mobile immigrants, meanwhile, had grown tired of living in a dense urban area where their tiny apartments were only steps from the family store. They strived for something different: a home in a newer neighborhood where work life and home life were separated both physically and emotionally, and their children did not have to play on cement. Milton Schwartz's family left for Northwest Baltimore in 1947. He recalls that greenery was a welcome contrast to life in the old neighborhood, where he had to walk ten blocks to see "a blade of grass if it didn't grow between a piece of cement."[39] Yet, something was lost in the move. Families might have crowded into tight quarters but, as Gail Davis recalls, sharing a room with her brother brought them closer. The streets might have seemed like inadequate playgrounds to ambitious parents or concerned reformers, but Jerome Sefret, who spent hours playing outside his parents' Lombard Street store with children of fellow shop owners, has only fond memories of the busy sidewalks. He still counts his Lombard Street playmates among his closest friends, more than half a century later.[40]

The children who came of age in the 1920s and 1930s were a transitional generation that bridged old world and new. As their parents learned English, familiarized themselves with American customs, and established themselves financially, they moved away from East Baltimore. Yet, they never lost their attachment to the old neighborhood. They cling to memories of their old haunts with a fierce and protective nostalgia, describing East Baltimore as a

Boys at play, 1930s.

JMM 1995.162.5a

good starter neighborhood, a place where a tightly knit immigrant community provided a safe foundation, where childhood could be lived in the space of a few blocks' radius, and where parents' aspirations for their offspring became reality. Louis Shecter relates the story of a conversation between his grandfather and an acquaintance he met in synagogue. It captures the sense of hope and expectation that sustained East Baltimore's Jewish residents: "My grandfather asked the man in front of him: 'How old are your sons?' The man's answer was, 'The doctor is four and the lawyer is two and a half.'"[41]

NOTES

The essay's title, "We Were Poor and We Didn't Know It," is excerpted from a comment made by Rena Kolman in her interview of May 18, 2006 (OH 684, Jewish Museum of Maryland). Lead quotations come from the following sources: Joseph Hirschmann interview, October 28, 1975, OH 28, Jewish Museum of Maryland [hereafter JMM]; Edward Attman interview, November 28, 2005, OH 678, JMM; Perry Siegel interview, May 1, 1988, OH 248, JMM; Isadore Livov and Norma Livov Wolod interview, June 7, 2006, OH 687, JMM; Gail Davis interview, June 29, 2006, OH 689, JMM.

1   Kolman interview.

2   Louis Shecter, "I Remember Shomri Shemerish," unpublished manuscript, n.d., MS 55, JMM.

3   Janet E. Kemp, *Housing Conditions in Baltimore* (Baltimore: The Federated Charities, 1907); Jewish Educational Alliance staff report, January 1921, Associated Jewish Community Federation papers, 1995.98.56, JMM; Kathryn Sollins and Dora Silber interview, December 7, 1980, OH 123, JMM.

4   Ida Marton interview, February 21, 1983, OH 177, JMM; Kemp, 13: "Fifty years ago this section was the home of many old Baltimore families of high social standing, who used, doubtless, to sit in the pleasant summer evenings on the fine old marble steps which are now occupied by the dark-eyed Jewish mothers with their babies, and around which older children play."

5   Kathryn Sollins interview, September 15, 1982, OH 154, JMM.

6   Avrum Rifman, "In My Mother's Court," *Generations* 1, no. 5 (December 1980): 40; Edward Attman interview; Jerome Sefret interview, June 8, 2007, OH 713, JMM.

7   U.S. Census Schedules for Baltimore City, 1900, 1920, and 1930.

8   Paul Wartzman interview, June 5, 2006, OH 162, JMM; Hymen Saye interview, OH 183, March 10, and March 16, 1983, JMM.

9   Eric Pernikoff interview, January 2, 2002, OH 516, JMM.

10 Hutchins Hapgood, cited in Irving Howe and Kenneth Libo, eds., *How We Lived: A Documentary History of Immigrant Jews in America, 1880-1930* (New York: Richard Marek Publishers, 1979), 45.

11 Case records for the Goldsmith family, Jewish Family and Children's Service Records, 1869-1973, MS 138, JMM.

12 Milton Schwartz interview, November 9, 2005, OH 676, JMM.

13 Morris Gordon interview, January 22, 1992, OH 269, JMM; Sollins and Silber interview; Sollins interview.

14 Saye interview.

15 On the topic of immigrant children and school see: Steven Mintz, *Huck's Raft: A History of American Childhood* (Cambridge: Harvard University Press, 2004), 204; Elliott West and Paula Petrick, eds., *Small Worlds: Children and Adolescents in America, 1850-1950* (Lawrence: University Press of Kansas, 1992), 44-45.

16 Charles Solomon interview, November 25, 1973, OH 18, JMM.

17 Henry Burke interview, May 6, 1986, OH 212, JMM; Irene Copinger, "Baltimore has a colorful old-world market," *Baltimore Sun*, April 13, 1924, 1.

18 Paul Goodman interview, September 28, 2005, OH 675, JMM.

19 Saye interview; Aaron Smelkinson interview, July 9, 2004, OH 620, JMM.

20 Davis interview; "Associated News: East Baltimore," *Baltimore Jewish Times*, April 5, 1929.

21 Sefret interview; *Baltimore City Directory* (Baltimore: R.L. Polk & Company, 1930).

22 Rifman, "In My Mother's Court," 40; Al Olschansky, "Baltimore City in its Heyday," *Generations* (Spring 1988): 10.

23 Wartzman interview.

24 Livov and Wolod interview.

25 Seymour Attman interview, September 20, 1982, OH 162, JMM.

26 Wartzman interview; Livov and Wolod interview.

27 Solomon interview; Livov and Wolod interview.

28 For comments about friendships (with both Jews and others), see Edward Attman, Seymour Attman, Livov and Wolod, and Saye interviews. Minnie Schneider, who was born in Russia in 1896 and settled in East Baltimore with her family at the age of five, states, "I never had a gentile friend. All my friends were always Jewish and I always kept within Jewish circles" (Minnie Schneider interview, May 21, 1977, OH 66, JMM). For comments about eating kosher food in other families' homes, see Shoshana Cardin interview, August-September 2001, OH 629, JMM.

29 Schwartz interview.

30 Rifman, "In My Mother's Court."

31 Wartzman interview; Schwartz interview.

32 The sanitary sewer system reached East Baltimore in the mid-1910s, but many building owners waited years more before they hooked up to it. See also Kemp, *Housing Conditions*; and "Report of the Federated Jewish Charities, 1913," cited in Isaac M. Fein, *The Making of an American Jewish Community: The History of Baltimore Jewry from 1773 to 1920* (Philadelphia: Jewish Publication Society of America, 1971), 160.

33 Unattributed quotation in Isaac Rehert, "Street corner club grows 50 years of friendship," *Baltimore Sun*, July 1, 1980.

34 "Jewish Educational Alliance," *Baltimore Jewish Times*, October 31, 1930, 36; Livov and Wolod interview.

35 Wartzman interview; JEA Director's Report, March 1920. Associated Jewish Community Federation papers, JEA scrapbook, 1995.098, JMM; Sefret interview.

36 JEA board notes, April 5, 1921, 1995.098, JMM; JEA staff report, January 1921, 1995.98.56, JMM.

37 Ibid.

38 Livov and Wolod interview; *Baltimore Building Low-Rent Homes* (Baltimore: Housing Authority of Baltimore City, 1939), 10. The booklet quotes a report presented to Mayor Howard W. Jackson in 1934, in which this language appears.

39 Milton Schwartz interview.

40 Davis interview; Sefret interview.

41 Louis Shecter, "I Remember Shomri Shemerish."

"Keeping Peace in the Family"

The Jewish Court of Arbitration,
1912-1945

A woman seeks a permit to erect a tombstone over her mother's grave, but the synagogue that owns the cemetery argues that the plot is actually owned by a relative—who is in a dispute with the congregation. No apology and no permit, so the woman goes to court.

A man signs a two-year lease on a store, only to discover that his competitors are members of an association that has pressured wholesalers not to sell to the new merchant. Caught between his landlord, who expects him to honor his lease, and his inability to stock his store, the man goes to court.

A Hebrew School believes that one of its employees is preparing meals for its students that are not strictly kosher. The cook denies this, and the Hebrew School goes to court.[1]

These cases—and hundreds more—were adjudicated by the Jewish Court of Arbitration, a fascinating yet little-known organization dedicated to "keeping peace in the family."[2] From 1914 to the beginning of World War II, the Jewish Court of Arbitration docketed nearly 600 cases, most of which originated in the immigrant community concentrated in East Baltimore. By the 1940s, the newcomers had largely acculturated, and the Court of Arbitration gradually declined. But during its heyday, the Court represented a singular response to the needs of an immigrant population—and the more established Jewish residents who had preceded them.

Both the Court itself, and the cases it resolved, reflect the concerns of Jewish Baltimore at a time when immigrants and their children were at an all-time peak as a proportion of the local community. A close reading of the sources provides insights into the everyday lives of the newcomers, the concerns of community leaders, and the adaptation of Jewish tradition to modern circumstances.[3]

"THE SPIRIT OF THE SYNAGOGUE": ORIGINS OF THE COURT

During the period of intense Jewish immigration from Eastern Europe between 1880 and 1914, waves of newcomers joined Baltimore's Jewish community: in 1880, an estimated 10,000 Jews lived in Baltimore, but by 1927, the number had risen to nearly 70,000. While the proportion of Baltimore Jews who were immigrants and their children is indeterminate, they were clearly a very substantial proportion of the resident population. The new immigrants brought with them a culture steeped in Yiddish and traditional religious practice. Arriving in America, they confronted radically different conditions that required continual adjustments, while the dislocations of migration presented an additional set of challenges.[4]

New circumstances demanded new responses. In 1909, Louis Levin, a prominent lawyer, writer, and social activist, published a column in Baltimore's *Jewish Comment* calling for the creation of a forum to which the city's Jewish residents could bring their concerns and differences, rather than airing their

"Keeping Peace in the Family": The Jewish Court of Arbitration, 1912-1945

BY MELANIE SHELL-WEISS

64

Melanie Shell-Weiss, Ph.D., is Visiting Assistant Professor of History, Johns Hopkins University.

OVERLEAF: *Lombard Street, circa 1930.*

Courtesy of the Peale Museum, JMM 1987.161.1

grievances in the City courts. "I do not mean a little Jewish court before which a few wranglers tell their stories to judges bound by rules and laws having no relation to these times," he wrote. "I mean some tribunal in which the spirit of the synagogue could be brought into authoritative play on the relations of everyday activities."[5]

While Levin's proposal produced no immediate result, three years later an unusual case arrived in the public courts. A Jewish worker claimed sick benefits for the week that he was sitting *shiva*, the traditional week of mourning.

Immigrants at a currency exchange booth at Locust Point, circa 1904.

Courtesy of The Maryland Historical Society

His Jewish employer rejected the claim, arguing that the ritual of sitting *shiva* was deserving of respect but did not entitle anyone to sick benefits that were to be used solely for illness. Countering that he was not feeling well at the time, the worker sued his employer. The case came before a gentile judge, John J. Dobler, who suggested to several Jewish attorneys that cases like this should not be heard in a City court, but rather in a Jewish venue.[6]

A number of variant versions of this story appear in subsequent accounts, but the outcome was decisive: several community leaders, representing both the more established "uptown" Jews and the newer "downtown" immigrants, joined together to organize a Court of Arbitration to settle "Jewish questions in a Jewish atmosphere, presided over by Jewish men who can understand the nature of problems more readily than a learned non-Jewish judge."[7]

The idea for a Jewish Court came at a time when collaboration was very much on the minds of many of Baltimore's Jewish community leaders, and this framed how the Court was formed and managed. Like the German-speaking Jews from Central Europe who had preceded them, and from whom they were separated by language and custom, the Eastern European immigrants had quickly established their own charitable organizations, congregations, and societies. By the first years of the twentieth century, Baltimore's Jewish organizations were effectively divided into "two distinct and independent" communities. Nowhere was this clearer than in the city's charitable organizations. The so-called "German" Jews ran their communal agencies under the rubric of the Federated Jewish Charities, which incorporated in 1906, while the "Russian" (Eastern European) Jews managed their constellation of agencies under the rubric of the United Hebrew Charities, which incorporated in 1908. As historian Isaac Fein notes, "The Federated and the United brought some order to the affairs of the community. . . . Both organizations worked for the same causes—sometimes in harmony, other times at cross purposes; and very often their work overlapped."[8]

Louis H. Levin had made it his particular mission to foster collaboration among the city's "German" and "Russian" Jews and their respective federations. Levin was from one of Baltimore's leading German-Jewish families and among the city's best-recognized citizens.[9] He began writing a weekly column on "civic problems" in the Baltimore *Jewish Comment* in 1895 and was also a regular contributor to the *Baltimore Sun*. In 1899 he became editor-in-chief of the *Jewish Comment*, a position that he held until 1916 and that he used to promote amalgamation of the "uptown" and "downtown" communities. As secretary of the Federated Jewish Charities through the 1910s, Levin proselytized the importance of "working together for the common good."[10] Therefore, when a meeting was convened to establish the Jewish Court of Arbitration, it was done as a cooperative effort. During its early years, the Court of Arbitration was officially a constituent agency of the United Hebrew Charities, the federation of the "downtown" Jewish community. However, its board of directors represented a mix of German and Eastern European

Louis Levin, circa 1915.
JMM 1987.80.2

Officers and Directors of United Hebrew Charities

Jewish interests. Two members each from the United Hebrew Charities, the Federated Jewish Charities, the Menorah Lodge of B'nai B'rith (German), and the Independent Order of B'rith Sholom (Russian) constituted the JCA board.[11]

By 1914, the Jewish Court of Arbitration was an active agency; it incorporated in 1920 and in 1921 the Court became an agency of the Associated Jewish Charities, Baltimore's newly founded amalgamation of German and Russian agencies.[12]

The officers and directors of the United Hebrew Charities, the association of "Russian" charities.

JMM 1996.7.1

"THE GOOD NAME OF THE JEW": INTENTIONS AND EXPECTATIONS

The Court's founders had several motives for establishing the JCA. One of their principal considerations was to ensure that complex and sometimes obscure issues of Jewish law, tradition, and ritual not be heard in non-Jewish courts that were incapable of understanding and deciding them. How was a public court to decide cases relating to *kashrut* or burial, religious divorce or synagogue practice? The fact that many newcomers did not speak English also worked to their disadvantage in public courts. In contrast, the Jewish Court of Arbitration would provide a sympathetic setting and knowledgeable adjudicators.[13]

The Jewish Court of Arbitration was also to be an instrument to avoid or

This portrait of the Reinhard family depicts a fashionable, well-to-do German-Jewish family of the early 1900s. By this time, Baltimore's German Jews were thoroughly Americanized and had achieved a high level of economic success.

JMM 1987.187.3

mitigate embarrassment for Jews in the gentile community. Again and again, the Court's leaders appealed to their constituents to employ the JCA rather than resort to City courts for resolution of disputes. "The aim of the Jewish Court is to carry out the Jewish ideal of justice . . . without the unpleasant publicity which accompanies court trials," argued one of the JCA officers.[14] Another referred to the "humiliation of having non-Jews, with no understanding or sympathy for Jewish customs, pass upon the merits or demerits of such cases."[15] S. Richard Nathanson, the longtime secretary of the Court, wrote in 1928 that one of the JCA's purposes was to "prevent 'rishes' [scandal] by having [religious] questions aired in legal courts presided over by non-Jews before non-Jewish juries."[16] And H.L. Caplan, the longtime JCA president, noted that cases "arising in public courts proved to be an embarrassment to the entire Jewish community."[17] In its self-styled "propaganda," the JCA was forthright in appealing to Jewish attorneys to recommend cases to the Court of Arbitration "if they feel that airing questions before non-Jewish judges would jeopardize the good name of the Jew."[18]

Given the antisemitic attitudes prevalent at that time, anxieties about "embarrassment" and "humiliation" were well-founded. Prejudicial stereotypes abounded: Jews were commonly characterized as shiftless, lazy, or incapable of assimilating. Job advertisements expressed a preference for "non-Jewish" employees, and more than one public school teacher criticized Jews' "natural deficiencies."[19] Concern about antisemitism coalesced with what we might term "status anxiety" on the part of the more established Jewish residents who feared that the great mass of newcomers would jeopardize their hard-won position in the community.

Still, the establishment and operation of the Jewish Court of Arbitration was also informed by idealism and a commitment to service. Maintaining harmony within the Jewish community had been a desideratum for millennia. Family squabbles, business disputes, and claims against synagogues, cemeteries, and other communal agencies were disruptive and inimical of traditional Jewish values. Within a minority community largely composed of "greenhorns," there were already enough shared challenges (and too few resources) to spend time and energy in lengthy intra-communal disputes. Maintaining *shalom* (peace) within the community was too pressing to leave to the discretion of aggrieved individuals.

The question then became: how to "settle Jewish questions in a Jewish atmosphere," simply, directly, efficiently, and decisively.

"Settling Jewish Questions in a Jewish Atmosphere": Precedents and Procedures

One of the initial pressures for creating the JCA came from cases involving Orthodox Jewish religious tradition. Most of the Eastern European newcomers, even those avowedly secularist, Zionist, and Socialist, hailed from communities where the values and traditions of the corporate community (*kahal*) were still strong. Many of the immigrants were Orthodox in their practice, and Yiddish was their everyday language.

As a result, JCA leaders linked their new enterprise to ancient Jewish tradition. JCA literature (or "propaganda," as they termed it) frequently alluded to the Mosaic Code and the Jewish tradition of communal responsibility. "The Jewish Court . . . has behind it the historical weight of the Sanhedrin, of the judges who thousands of years ago administered the law and ruled over the children of Israel," wrote one JCA leader. Pains were taken to consult with rabbis on religious issues. Rabbi Abraham Schwartz, perhaps the city's most respected Orthodox authority, was a frequent adviser. Yet, at the same time, the JCA touted its thoroughly "modern" approach, its lay judges (in contrast to rabbinic authority), and its reliance on good business sense and equity rather than on Jewish legal codes. In short, the JCA styled itself as an amalgam of old traditions and new practices.[20]

The Court's structure was loosely modeled on the tradition of the *Bet Din* (literally, "a house of judgment"), a traditional community tribunal

Toba and Mendel Lerner. Eastern European immigrants differed from the assimilated Jews who had arrived before the 1880s in custom, style, and religious observance.

Gift of Morton H. Weiner, JMM 2005.5.2

where Jews brought their differences before a rabbi and had their cases heard. Such tribunals were common in small communities across Eastern Europe and grew directly from even older traditions in ancient Israel. The Book of Exodus reports that Moses served as a magistrate for the Israelites, and later Biblical references show that he delegated judicial authority to appointed "chiefs." By the first centuries of the Common Era, rabbinic authorities had developed a complex system of courts that dealt with both civil and criminal law, guided and informed by authorized judges. Throughout the Middle Ages and into the modern period of Jewish history, Jewish courts of law were a central feature of the *kahal*, the autonomous and largely self-governing Jewish community.[21]

Several features of the traditional *Bet Din* carried over into the new Jewish Court of Arbitration. One was the importance of turning to a Jewish court rather than a gentile one, partly in response to community pressure and partly to avoid "aggrandizing the honor of alien gods." A second feature was the emphasis on arbitrating disputes, an effort to compose differences for the sake of peace. In civil cases, traditional Jewish courts required three judges (often the lead judge, a rabbi, would appoint two lay people to sit with him in judgment), so the JCA also adopted a system of three judges. Jewish courts had jurisdiction not only over individuals, but also over the community (*kahal*) when individuals had claims against it—a tradition that the JCA maintained, when it considered cases involving congregations and other community agencies.[22]

Those who failed to abide by the findings of the traditional *Bet Din* knew that they could be sanctioned by the community and banished from religious connections, even if they did not risk imprisonment or other formal legal penalties. In Baltimore, the Jewish Court of Arbitration required that the disputants sign a binding agreement to abide by the decision of the arbitrators—a precaution that ensured that JCA decisions were generally accepted by both the plaintiff and the defendant.[23]

Although its leadership acknowledged JCA links to tradition, they also stressed that the JCA was a thoroughly "modern" organization and was "in no sense a religious tribunal." Instead, the founders maintained, "apart from the faith of the largest number of its patrons and the occasional use of Yiddish, the only thing reminiscent of its Jewish up-bringing is that three laymen preside as judges." One additional feature is notable: the JCA excluded attorneys from serving as judges, though they could be consulted as experts should the lay judges deem this appropriate.[24]

Whether their backgrounds were "German" or "Russian," the JCA founders and officers shared a concern that "antiquated customs" were (or could be) a source of embarrassment for the Jewish community as a whole. While the JCA effectively adjudicated cases involving Orthodox congregations, organizations, and individuals, its leadership occasionally fulminated against specific rituals and customs, arguing that they had outlived their times. In September 1930, for instance, JCA Secretary Nathanson published

Rabbi Abraham Schwartz.
Gift of Stuart R. Rombro, JMM 1976.1.1

The Talmud Torah Hall on East Baltimore Street, first home of the Jewish Court of Arbitration.

Gift of Earl Pruce, JMM 1985.90.13

an article in the *Baltimore Jewish Times* objecting to the persistence of rituals such as the *get* and *halitzah*, which he described as "ancient customs that are altogether obsolete and [that] Modern Israel can very well do without."[25]

The JCA succeeded in resolving many of the cases brought before it, quickly and cheaply. The process was quite simple. The plaintiff requested a hearing, paid a nominal fee for delivery of papers to the other party, and the case was promptly heard by a three-man panel that met in the heart of East Baltimore (first at the Baltimore Talmud Torah and later at the Jewish Educational Alliance). Prior to the hearing, each of the disputants signed an agreement to abide by the Court's decision and swore an oath to be truthful, while wearing a traditional *kipah*, or yarmulke. Each party to the dispute then told his or her side of the story, witnesses were called, the judges deliberated, and a decision was rendered.[26]

A theme that ran through JCA proceedings was the quest for *shalom* (peace or harmony) in the community. As a result, many of the cases brought to the JCA were actually resolved through the good auspices of the JCA secretary before ever arriving at the Court, either by counseling of the

For many years, the JCA was based at the Jewish Educational Alliance on East Baltimore Street.

JMM 1995.189.429

aggrieved party or by informal mediation. Community members were as likely to knock on the door of individual board members at home to seek advice about problems or potential cases, as to go to the Court's official office. "Records on paper hardly show the amount of work and effort required to follow up, interview clients, and even make visits to congregations to bring about amicable understanding," Nathanson wrote in the Court's 1930 annual report. "Clients call at home, office, as well as the Jewish Educational Alliance."[27] Unlike City courts, which were shrouded in formality and set apart from the community at large, the Jewish Court of Arbitration was dedicated to the resolution of disputes through counseling, mediation, and arbitration.

When cases did reach the Court, decisions were frequently compromises intended to leave both parties with a sense of satisfaction. In 1918, for example, a customer claimed to have given a supplier a twenty-dollar note instead of a ten-dollar note in payment for his milk bill. Since there were no witnesses, the judges could not be certain about the denomination of the note. So they split the difference, ruling that the milkman should return five dollars to his client.[28]

The judges followed a similar course of action in a case brought against a kosher butcher. A patron bought meat that was promised to be kosher. But when the patron got the meat home, he realized it lacked any rabbi's stamp. Fearing the meat was *treyf* (not kosher) the patron took the issue before the Jewish Court. He asked not only that the judges investigate the butcher's business practices but also that the butcher reimburse him for the cost of his pots and pans along with the cost of the meat, as his utensils had been soiled by their contact with *treyf* meat. The butcher countered that the meat had previously borne the stamp, but when the fat was removed, the seal was also cut off. In this case, too, the Court aimed toward fairness rather than a narrow definition of "right" and "wrong." Arguing that there was insufficient proof that the meat sold was not kosher, the court declined to award damages to the patron. But they did encourage the butcher to reimburse his customer for the cost of the meat itself. In so doing, they preserved the reputation and livelihood of the kosher butcher, while also striving to placate a disgruntled patron.[29]

A similar spirit of compromise is evidenced in a case that a rabbi brought against a matchmaker for claiming false credit for the marriage of a local couple. Noting that it was he who had introduced the couple, the rabbi argued that he, not the matchmaker, was entitled to the $125 matchmaking fee. The matchmaker countered, however, that only he knew of the prospective groom's desire to get married. Thus, because the matchmaker conveyed that information to the bride's family, he deserved full credit and compensation for the match. Again, the judges decided upon a compromise. "Inasmuch as the plaintiff was instrumental in producing the groom to the defendant, and we find that it was through said introduction that the defendant came to know that the young man was open for a marriage proposition," the judges wrote, "we therefore find that the plaintiff is entitled to one-third of the commission from the introduction as without the same, the defendant would not have been in a position to make a match." The remaining two-thirds of the marriage fee was paid to the matchmaker.[30]

Again and again, the JCA judges struggled to resolve disputes in a way that would close the matter definitively. Compromise was their preferred approach, and such decisions went a long way toward forging community among the city's diverse Jewish residents in a critical period of rapid transformation.

A summons to appear before the Jewish Court of Arbitration.

Jewish Board of Arbitration Collection, JMM

No. 0160
Summoned Benj. Schiffman 13 N. Caroline St
On 11/11/19

Bailiff.

"A Court Where the Humblest Can Feel at Ease": A Mirror of Everyday Life

The JCA's founders, officers, and directors were assiduous in promoting the Court as a central agency of community in Jewish Baltimore. They secured coverage in the Jewish and general press, as well as in specialist publications, submitted glowing annual reports to the Associated Jewish Charities, and leafleted local Jewish attorneys.[31] Despite their persistent advocacy (and somewhat extravagant claims), the Jewish Court of Arbitration docketed only a modest number of cases each year—an average of just over twenty cases annually for nearly thirty years—many of which were either refused jurisdiction by the defendant or settled informally before they reached the JCA judges.[32] However, even the limited number of cases that are documented in the JCA records reflect the everyday life of the Baltimore Jewish community during the interwar years.

As a rule, the Court refused to take on domestic disputes, which tended to be handled either by civil or religious authorities. Nevertheless, over the years various domestic cases were docketed, though they were frequently disposed of by the JCA secretary without ever coming to the Court for arbitration. In 1931, for instance, a family could not agree on how to care for an aging parent. The Court did whatever it could to avoid interceding, arguing that it would be far better for the siblings if they could agree on how to settle their own family's affairs in private. "We would appreciate your calling to see the Secretary for the purpose of talking things over with a possibility of straightening out this family misunderstanding and to relieve any feelings that may now exist between the sons, daughters, and mother," the chair of the Board wrote. When one of the brothers refused to respond to the Court's requests to speak with his sisters, the Board declined to hear the case.[33]

A few years later the Court heard from a daughter who complained that her brothers would not provide any assistance whatsoever for their ailing mother. Again the judges urged the family to do what they could to settle their differences privately. They encouraged the brothers to work out how to provide for their mother "without having a social organization to intercede." However, the judges continued, "if you cannot agree among yourselves, then we are willing to assist in calling a hearing and decide just what you boys ought to do for your mother."[34]

Constant movement—to Baltimore from Europe, from Baltimore to other parts of the United States and within Baltimore from one neighborhood to another—created dislocations. Cases docketed by the Court reflect the sometimes harsh realties of migration. In one instance, individuals who had entrusted funds to middlemen (who promised to get those monies to relatives in Russia) appealed to the Court when the middlemen proved dishonest, and the monies never reached their families back home.[35]

Cases of desertion suggest the instability of a dynamic, changing community. In one notable 1923 case, the JCA uncovered an instance of serial desertion in which a man abandoned a family in Russia, then left his family in Baltimore, and eventually settled down with yet a third family in San Francisco.[36] In contrast, the Court provided recourse for men who were overtaxed by demands of support from estranged spouses or children. In 1916, Lena Kalamanowitz left her husband, Louis. Some months later she returned and petitioned him to move in with her again. Louis moved back in, but he balked at the requirement that he continue to provide for her financially. The judges ruled that because Lena had left Louis, rather than the other way around, she was not entitled to any support. They also suggested that Louis move out from under her roof. Both Mr. and Mrs. Kalamanowitz were satisfied with the ruling.[37]

Business complaints relating to matters such as labor disputes, conflict between customers and proprietors, or demand of payment for services rendered were common throughout the life of the Jewish Court. Customers who were angry that a publicly distributed advertising circular "misrepresented certain key facts" or who purchased goods that were not as promised brought their grievances to the Court. In one case, a Broadway fishmonger

Although the W.S. Woolen Mills Company was not among the litigants, such garment industry firms appeared frequently on the JCA docket.

Gift of Jerome D. Buxbaum, JMM 1998.165.1

These two East Baltimore Street establishments, Livov Bros. Furriers and the Esterson Neckwear Company, did not appear before the JCA, but they are typical of the small family businesses that made up a considerable portion of the Court's cases.

LEFT: Courtesy of Isadore Livov, JMM L2006.22.7
RIGHT: JMM CP12.2007.1

docketed a complaint against his supplier, who had allowed barrels of herring to sit in the hot sun and spoil because they were not delivered to him on time.[38]

In a community of newcomers, many of whom lived precarious lives, small disagreements loomed large, especially when they revolved around money. Benny Blaustein filed a complaint against Morris Yospin in order to settle a problem of business competition. Blaustein had purchased his store at 636 South Washington Street from Yospin, on the condition that Yospin would not open a new establishment within five surrounding blocks to avoid competition. Within a matter of months, however, Yospin did open a new store, just three blocks away, violating their original contract.[39] In a parallel case, Joseph Grossman and Michael Heller, both paper carriers for a Yiddish newspaper, got into a dispute over where one man's territory began and the other's ended. To resolve the matter, the judges created a house-by-house chart to evaluate just where the majority of Jewish residents were living in East Baltimore in order to ensure that each man could earn a living.[40]

In a community deeply engaged in the clothing and textile trades, garment industry disputes of all kinds came to the JCA. Wolf Levin, a skilled tailor who was forced to miss work for four weeks due to a serious illness, successfully brought a suit against the Custom Tailors Sick Benefits and Relief Association to collect his full benefits for time lost from work.[41] Another plaintiff brought a complaint against a man he had paid to teach his son the cutter's trade, a

relatively skilled occupation. The Court found that "the fault has been the principal's in not being adept or cut out for that sort of work," and, with the cooperation of the defendant, $75 was returned to the plaintiff.[42]

Disputes over property, loans and mortgages, salaries and fees cover a spectrum of cases. In 1926, a dispute over payment of a mortgage arose between Jacob Zalis and attorney Michael Miller. Miller claimed Zalis owed money to a building association. Zalis, however, claimed no responsibility for the loan because he had turned the money over to his son Joel, who had moved to Miami, Florida. So the Zalis family enlisted the help of the Jewish Court of Arbitration to help settle the case.[43]

In a very different kind of case, two neighbors, Wolf Singer and Abraham Weimer, appeared before the Court to discuss the issue of a fence between their adjoining properties. Mr. Weimer began building a fence without consulting Mr. Singer. After putting in 110 of the roughly 200 total posts, Weimer approached Singer and asked him to pay for one-half of the total cost of the fence. Singer refused. Unable to reach an agreement, the two men

Congregation Anshe Sphard, 1937. The JCA frequently heard disputes involving Jewish communal institutions.

JMM 1987.137.1

brought their case before the Court. The judges ruled that as Mr. Singer was not consulted, Mr. Weimer should pay the full cost of the 110 posts. But the men should split the cost of the remaining eighty-five posts evenly between the two of them.[44]

Some of the business disputes brought before the Court involved specifically Jewish services to the community. Wolf Kushner, for instance, brought a complaint against Mr. S. Weinstein when Weinstein refused to pay him for the Hebrew lessons Kushner was giving to Weinstein's son. In another case, a man brought in his *tefillin* for repair, but the repairman lost the *tefillin* and was consequently required by the Court to reimburse his customer.[45] In another case, a widow complained that a local undertaker had failed to prepare her husband's body according to Orthodox custom.[46]

One of the most important categories of JCA cases—essentially a special niche—involved disputes between individuals and Jewish organizations. In situations where the JCA arbitrated issues involving community agencies, the Court approximated the traditional authority of the *Bet Din*, a virtually unprecedented role in modern America. In one case, Israel Steinberg brought a claim against the Eden Street Synagogue for work he had performed in its cemetery. The JCA ruled that the plaintiff was owed $12.10—and split the cost among no fewer than five Jewish organizations that used the cemetery. The H.L. Caplan Company brought suit in the JCA against a neighboring congregation, seeking to compel the synagogue to demolish a "spite" wall between their properties. Henry Goodman left his watch as security with the Hebrew Free Loan Society. When he went to redeem it, Goodman discovered that the Society had sold it. The JCA judges required the Society to reimburse Mr. Goodman, but expressed "a sense of simpathy [*sic*] to [the plaintiff] and not in penalty to the association."[47]

Disputes between congregations and their erstwhile employees were also a JCA staple. In one case, Mr. Cohen was hired by a board member of a shul to serve as sexton for its cemetery. After Cohen was employed for one week, however, the congregation was not satisfied with his work and decided to fire him. Cohen felt the firing was unfair and appealed to the Jewish Court. The judges ruled in favor of the congregation and supported the decision to fire Mr. Cohen.[48]

A cantor made a contract with a Baltimore congregation for services over the High Holy Days. His fee was 600 dollars. But the congregation was singularly unimpressed with the cantor's performance on Rosh Hashanah and Yom Kippur. The cantor then became sick "either accidentally or purposely" on the last two days of Succoth. So, the congregation decided to pay him only 400 dollars. The cantor appealed to the Jewish Court. Likewise, a Hebrew teacher claimed ten days of salary for time spent in orientations at a Talmud Torah. In the former case, the JCA judges effected a compromise, but in the latter case, the judges ruled that no salary was due the new teacher as the time spent was to "acquaint him with his duties."[49]

Issues between congregations and members could be particularly sticky. Isaac Rosensweig demanded that his congregation reimburse him for two pews and, five years later, another member of the same congregation asked that a pledge of fifty dollars for the purchase of *yahrzeit* (memorial) lights be nullified, since he was estranged from the congregation and was not going to make use of them.[50] In one of the most widely known and most complex cases of intra-congregational squabbles—that of a congregation at a Jewish farming colony near Ellicott City—the JCA intervened, mediated, and monitored the situation for several years.[51]

Disputes about permits to erect tombstones in local cemeteries represented a particularly touchy and emotional set of issues. Usually the complaint was that the synagogue or cemetery was trying to extort from distraught relatives an unreasonable fee for permitting erection of a tombstone on a family member's grave. Within just a few months, Benjamin Naiman complained about Anshei Neisen Congregation, and Louis Applefeld brought the JCA a dispute with Kneseth Israel Anshe Sfard.[52] In one instance, the plaintiff

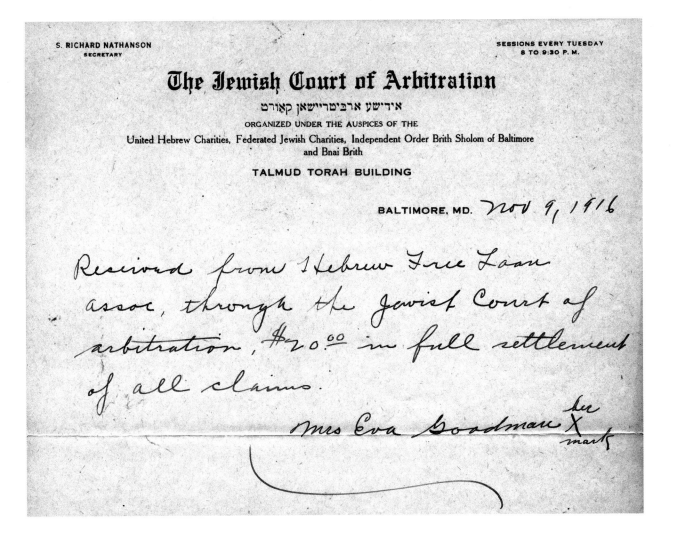

S. RICHARD NATHANSON
SECRETARY

SESSIONS EVERY TUESDAY
8 TO 9:30 P. M.

The Jewish Court of Arbitration

אידישע ארביטריישאן קאורט

ORGANIZED UNDER THE AUSPICES OF THE

United Hebrew Charities, Federated Jewish Charities, Independent Order Brith Sholom of Baltimore and Bnai Brith

TALMUD TORAH BUILDING

BALTIMORE, MD. *Nov 9, 1916*

Received from Hebrew Free Loan assoc, through the Jewish Court of arbitration, $20.00 in full settlement of all claims.

Mrs Eva Goodman her X mark

insulted the officials involved, making the case particularly nasty.[53] Typically the JCA judges issued compromise decisions, generally lowering the required fees but ensuring at least some payment to the cemetery.

Although the JCA served repeatedly as a peacemaker between and within Jewish organizations, few of these disputes involved traditional Jewish law or religious practices. Those kinds of cases tended to be passed along to rabbinic authorities, whose knowledge and prestige held sway in their communities.[54] The JCA cases were generally "business" issues involving money, property, and personal reputation. Although the type of specifically "Jewish" disputes the JCA addressed were quite different from those envisioned by its founders, over subsequent decades the JCA did keep a substantial number of potentially "embarrassing" cases out of the public courts, helping thereby to "protect the name of the Jew" and contributing to communal stability.

Small cemeteries, such as Anshe Neisin's, were involved in many contentious issues that came before the JCA. Anshe Neisin Cemetery is part of Rosedale, Baltimore's largest Jewish cemetery complex, pictured here.

Photo by Jennifer Vess

80

Epilogue

By the end of World War II, the Eastern European immigrant community had successfully acculturated, and the Jewish Court of Arbitration's role had declined. By then, the number of cases heard annually had slowed to a trickle.[55] In an effort to reinvent itself, the Jewish Court of Arbitration changed its name to the Jewish Board of Arbitration in 1945. While the function of the Jewish Court remained largely unchanged, the new name aimed to emphasize its role as a sounding board for Jewish affairs rather than as an alternative to the city's legislative system.

Still, the organization continued its decline. One of the last cases heard before the Court in 1949 focused on a diamond ring, given by Jack Kiper to his sister-in-law, Edith Cooper, at the time Mr. Kiper arrived in the United States from Germany. After sponsoring Mr. Kiper's migration to the United States, a necessity in order for him to secure a visa, Mrs. Cooper sold the ring "to raise funds for financial reasons." The Court ruled in favor of Mrs. Cooper, noting that since "the ring in question was presented 'for keeps' by Mr. Kiper," it was Mrs. Cooper's right to do with the ring as she saw fit.[56]

As the Jewish community moved north and west, the Jewish Board of Arbitration followed, relocating along with Baltimore Hebrew College to Park Heights in 1959 and meeting there exclusively.[57] In 1976, under the direction of Stanley Sollins, the Jewish Board of Arbitration became the Jewish Mediation and Arbitration Board, a part of the Baltimore Jewish Council, and met as needed in the offices of the Associated Jewish Charities on West Mount Royal Avenue. By the early 1980s, the Board had all but disappeared.

One last attempt was made to resurrect the JCA. In 1994, attorney Abba David Poliakoff proposed rejuvenating the Board of Arbitration to help resolve a number of messy public disputes involving public figures and institutions. Poliakoff believed that the Board could provide a forum to peacefully address these issues without litigation. "With everything that was happening, that is where I got the idea," Poliakoff recalled. "Wouldn't it be nice if we had a forum to be able to resolve these disputes outside of the public eye?"[58]

Although there were some who questioned whether the city still needed a Jewish arbitration board at all, Poliakoff countered that even if it were never used, it was critical to the community to have such a body. He won the support of the Associated Jewish Federation. The Board now has a new name, Jewish Arbitration and Mediation Board, and a new Board of Directors that, like the original Jewish Court of Arbitration, is composed of prominent attorneys, business people, physicians, and political figures.[59] Despite the involvement of these notables, the JAMB has yet to hear a case.

NOTES

The author gratefully acknowledges the helpful guidance of Avi Decter, Anita Kassof, and Deb Weiner. Their editing has made this chapter far stronger. The research assistance provided by Erin Titter and Jonathan Roscoe was also invaluable. I thank them all.

1   The first two instances are cited in "The Jewish Court of Arbitration," typescript, December 21, 1928, p. 2, Folder 25, Box 3, MS 4, Jewish Board of Arbitration Collection (hereafter JBA), Jewish Museum of Maryland (hereafter JMM) . The third is found in "Hebrew Parochial School v. Ellen Kanow," 1940, Folder 11, Box 1, JBA. The name of the organization was changed from the "Jewish Court of Arbitration" to the "Jewish Board of Arbitration" in 1945, and the archival materials are found under JBA.

2   Despite its long history in Baltimore Jewish life, to date only a single article has been published that documents the Jewish Court of Arbitration. See Lauraine Levy Kartman, "The Jewish Board of Arbitration in Baltimore, The Early Years," *Maryland Historical Magazine* 79, No. 4 (Winter 1984): 332-338. An unpublished manuscript also charts a portion of the Court's history. See Millie Kessler Caplan, "Jewish Court of Arbitration," Research Seminar Paper, Department of History, The Johns Hopkins University, December 1982, Folder 35, MS 119, Rifman Family Papers, JMM. The number of cases actually addressed by the Jewish Court of Arbitration is uncertain. In their "propaganda" pieces and annual reports, JCA officials repeatedly gave out very high numbers, and these have generally been taken at face value. For example, around 1926 George A. Rosette wrote in the *Baltimore Jewish Times* that "since its inception, [the JCA] has adjudicated over a thousand difficult cases out of court" ("The Jewish Court of Arbitration," Folder 27, Box 3, JBA). Similar figures are cited in Henry M. Hyde, "Lawyers Absent as Jewish Court Hears Dispute," *Baltimore Evening Sun,* February 13, 1925. However, the JCA Docket Book, 1916-1944, lists a total of 588 cases, just over twenty cases per year. The Docket Book was kept for decades by one man, JCA Secretary S. Richard Nathanson. The Docket Book lists many cases of disputes settled out of court or where the defendant refused to appear and the docket fee was returned to the plaintiff. This suggests that the Docket Book is a complete and accurate record of the cases dealt with by the Court and that the JCA annual reports and propaganda padded the numbers.

3   The emphasis on Jewish-American identity as the melding of older traditions with the new has been the focus of much recent scholarship. See Jenna Weissman Joselit, *The Wonders of America: Reinventing Jewish Culture, 1880-1950* (New York: Hill and Wang, 1994); Ewa Morawska, *Insecure Prosperity: Small-Town Jews in Industrial America, 1890-1940* (Princeton: Princeton University Press, 1996); Riv-Ellen Prell, *Fighting to Become Americans: Jews, Gender, and the Anxiety of Assimilation* (Boston: Beacon Press, 1999); and Daniel Soyer, *Jewish Immigrant Associations and American Identity in New York, 1880-1939* (Cambridge: Harvard University Press, 1997).

4   Isaac M. Fein, *The Making of an American Jewish Community: The History of Baltimore Jewry from 1773 to 1920* (Philadelphia: Jewish Publication Society of America, 1971), 141-224. Fein (149) estimates 10,000 Jews resident in Baltimore in 1880; the *American Jewish Yearbook 1930-1931* (Philadelphia: Jewish Publication Society, 1930) estimates 68,000 Jews in Baltimore in 1927 (223). The *American Jewish Yearbook 1917-1918* (Philadelphia: Jewish Publication Society, 1917) estimates 40,000 Jews in Baltimore in 1910, of whom at least 27,000 claimed Yiddish as their mother tongue or were children of Yiddish speakers (412-413).

5   *Jewish Comment,* December 10, 1909, 151.

6   H. L. Caplan, "Open Letter to Jewish Lawyers of Baltimore," n.d., Folder 25, Box 3, JBA. See also, *Jewish Comment,* n.d., Folder 25, Box 3, JBA.

7   Pamphlet, Jewish Board of Arbitration, n.d., Folder 25, Box 3, JBA.

8   Fein, *The Making of an American Jewish Community,* 216.

9   Louis Levin was born in Charleston, South Carolina, in 1866 to German-Jewish parents. They relocated to Baltimore in 1876. He graduated from college at age 15 and later attended law school at the Baltimore University School of Law. His wife, Bertha, was the youngest sister of Hadassah founder Henrietta Szold. See "Louis H. Levin," Vertical Files, JMM; J. Vincent Scarpaci, "Louis H. Levin of Baltimore: A Pioneer in Cultural Pluralism," *Maryland Historical Magazine* 77, No. 2 (June 1982): 183-192; Alexandra Lee Levin, *Dare to Be Different: A Biography of Louis H. Levin, A Sequel to The Szolds of Lombard Street* (New York: Bloch Publishing Company, 1972), xi, 6-24.

10   Louis H. Levin, "President's Address," *Third Joint Report: Federated Jewish Charities of Baltimore and Constituent Societies* (1910), 4-5, JMM 1990.199.

11   Solomon Ginsberg, President's Address, *Annual Joint Report: United Hebrew Charities of Baltimore and Constituent Organizations* (1917), 7, JMM 1991.85.1.

12   Caplan, "Jewish Court of Arbitration," 13.

13   "Open Letter to Jewish Lawyers of Baltimore," circa 1927, Folder 25, Box 3, JBA; and "The Jewish Court of Arbitration," Circular, February 26, 1917, Folder 25, Box 3, JBA.

14   Untitled, undated statement, Folder 27, Box 3, JBA.

15   "The Jewish Court of Arbitration," undated typescript, Folder 25, Box 3, JBA.

16   S. Richard Nathanson, "Jewish Court of Arbitration," *Baltimore Jewish Times,* March 14, 1928.

17   H.L. Caplan, "The Jewish Court of Arbitration," *Baltimore Jewish Times,* November 26, 1927.

18 "The Jewish Court of Arbitration," Circular, February 26, 1917; S. Richard Nathanson, "Jewish Court of Arbitration," undated typescript, Folder 25, Box 3, JBA.

19 William P. Dillingham, *Reports of the Immigration Commission: Dictionary of Races or Peoples, Vol. 5* (Washington: Government Printing Office, 1911), 6, 115, 126-128, 131-140; John Higham, *Strangers in the Land: Patterns of American Nativism, 1860-1925* (New Brunswick, N.J.: Rutgers University Press, 1988), 164-166. On Baltimore, see also Simon E. Sobeloff correspondence, 1923-1924, "Jewish Court of Arbitration and Anti-Defamation League" Folder, Box 358, Simon E. Sobeloff Papers, Manuscripts and Records Division, Library of Congress.

20 "The Jewish Court of Arbitration," undated typescript, Folder 25, Box 3, JBA. See also Hyde, "Lawyers Absent As Jewish Court Hears Disputes"; Rosette, "The Jewish Court of Arbitration."

21 Haim Hermann Cohn and Isaac Levitats, "Bet Din and Judges," and Isaac Levitats, "Community," *Encyclopaedia Judaica*, Second Edition (Detroit: Thomson Gale, 2007).

22 Ibid.

23 "Rules and Regulations of the Jewish Court of Arbitration of Baltimore" (1928), Box 3, JBA.

24 B.H. Hartogensis, "A Successful Community Court," *Journal of American Judicature Society*, typescript, Folder 27, Box 3, JBA; Nathanson, "Jewish Court of Arbitration," undated typescript; Hyde, "Lawyers Absent as Jewish Court Hears Dispute."

25 S. Richard Nathanson, "An Antiquated Custom in Practice," *Baltimore Jewish Times*, September 22, 1930. A *get* is a Jewish divorce. *Halitzah* is the biblically-prescribed ritual performed to release a childless widow from the Judaic law that required her to marry her deceased husband's brother.

26 "Rules and Regulations of the Jewish Court of Arbitration."

27 Jewish Court of Arbitration, "Report for the Year: 1930," JBA; "JCA/ADL" Folder, Box 358, Sobeloff Papers.

28 Rubin Ades v. Harry Ichikoff, August 6, 1918, Folder 7, Box 1, JBA; A. S. Wagner v. Jas. Morganstern and Son and I. W. Davidson Transportation Co., May 28, 1918, Folder 7, Box 1, JBA.

29 Morris Rosenburg v. K. Rosen and son, January 22, 1918, Box 1, JBA; "Jewish Court of Arbitration Helpful," Folder 25, Box 3, JBA.

30 S. R. Nathanson to Joseph H. Mellen, January 22, 1929, Folder 12, Box 1, JBA.

31 *Baltimore American*, August 24, 1918; *Baltimore Sun*, December 10, 1916; *Baltimore Sun*, December, 1923; *Jewish Morning Journal*, January 3, 1917; *Baltimore Jewish Times*, 1917 (Clippings, Folder 10, Box 1, JBA). Also *Baltimore Jewish Times*, March 2, 1928; Hartogensis, "A Successful Community Court"; "Open Letter to Jewish Lawyers of Baltimore," circa 1927, Folder 25, Box 3, JBA; "The Jewish Court of Arbitration," Circular.

32 Docket Book, Box 3, JBA.

33 S. R. Nathanson to Raymond Franklin, October 9, 1931, Folder 8, Box 1, JBA; Friedel Family Case File, 1932-1934, Folder 8, Box 1, JBA.

34 S. R. Nathanson to Harry Feinstein, December 26, 1947, Folder 8, Box 1, JBA.

35 S. R. Nathanson to Max Golditch, July 13, 1932, Folder 8, Box 1, JBA.

36 Mathilde Finkelstein, Eureka Benevolent Society, Federation of Jewish Charities of San Francisco, to S. R. Nathanson, November 27, 1923, Folder 7, Box 1, JBA. From Folder 5, Box 1, JBA: witness statement, "Witness to Jewish Wedding Ceremony of Jacob and Anna Berman, 1895"; Nathanson to Mrs. Anna Berman, September 23, 1929; Nathanson to Miss Nathalie Blockman, Eureka Benevolent Society, August 5, 1929; Miss Nathalie Blockman to Nathanson, September 18, 1929; Nathanson to Mrs. Anna Berman, September 23, 1929; Nathanson to Mrs. Anna Berman, January 16, 1931; Nathanson to Mrs. Morris Steinberg, January 9, 1931.

37 Louis Kalmanowitz v. Mrs. Lena Kalmanowitz, September 20, 1917, Folder 17, Box 2, JBA.

38 H. L. Caplan Co. v. Wolf Levin, July 10, 1917, Folder 1, Box 2, JBA.

39 S. Richard Nathanson to Morris Yospin, January 29, 1931, Folder 5, Box 1, JBA.

40 S. Richard Nathanson to Myer Levy, agent, *Jewish Morning Journal*, December 8, 1937, Folder 10, Box 1, JBA.

41 Wolf Levin v. Custom Tailors Sick Benefits and Relief Association, August 15, 1917, Folder 17, Box 2, JBA.

42 Hyman Caplan v. Mark Dischler, August 17, 1926, Docket Book, Box 3, JBA.

43 S. Richard Nathanson to Joel C. Zalis, Miami, Florida, December 24, 1926, Folder 12, Box 1, JBA; Michael Miller to S. Richard Nathanson, January 8, 1927, Folder 12, Box 1, JBA.

44 Decision, Wolf Singer v. Abraham Weimer, May 17, 1932, Folder 21, Box 2, Folder 21, JBA.

45 *Tefillin* are small leather boxes containing passages of scripture, worn on the arm and head during morning prayer. Wolf Kushner v. S. Weinstein, October 20, 1933, Folder 11, Box 2, JBA.

46 Annie Weintraub v. Jack Lewis, May 10, 1931, Docket Book, Box 3, JBA.

47 Israel Steinberg v. Eden Street Synagogue (Aitz Chiam) [sic], January 15, 1917, Docket Book, Box 3, JBA. H.L. Caplan Co. v. Kneseth Israel Anshe Sfard Congregation, November 5, 1931, Docket Book, Box 3, JBA. Henry Goodman v. Hebrew Free Loan Society, October 25, 1916, Docket Book, Box 3, JBA.

48 "Outstanding Religious Questions Settled at the Jewish Court: 1931," Folder 25, Box 3, JBA.

49 "Outstanding Religious Questions Settled"; Leon Frank v. West End Talmud Torah, August 1, 1916, Docket Book, Box 3, JBA.

50 Isaac Rosensweig v. Ansa Sfard [sic], February 1, 1921, Docket Book, Box 3, JBA; Wolf Moly v. Kneseth Israel Anshe Sfard, August 17, 1926, Docket Book, Box 3, JBA.

51 H. L. Caplan, "The Jewish Court of Arbitration," *Baltimore Jewish Times*, November 26, 1927, Folder 25, Box 3, JBA. S. Richard Nathanson to Beth Israel Anshei Sford Congregation, December 22, 1925; Nathanson to Mr. Wolf Singer, November 16, 1925; and Michael Miller to Nathanson, November 13, 1925, all Folder 5, Box 1, JBA. "Jewish Court of Arbitration Acts as Peacemaker in Communal Disagreement among Ellicott City Jews," *Baltimore Jewish Times*, n.d., Folder 25, Box 3, JBA.

52 Benjamin Naiman v. Anshei Neisen Congregation, November 22, 1926, and Louis Applefeld v. Kneseth Israel Anshe Sfard Congregation, June 22, 1926, Docket Book, Box 3, JCA.

53 "Outstanding Religious Questions Settled."

54 Notes on cases and "Case Examples," n.d., Folder 3, Box 1, JBA.

55 Budget Request Statements, 1939-1950, Folder 2, Box 1, JBA.

56 Jack Kiper v. Edith Cooper, September 22, 1949, Folder 23, Box 2, JBA.

57 "Cornerstone to be Laid for Hebrew College," *Baltimore Evening Sun*, October 4, 1957, Vertical File, JMM; "Baltimore Hebrew College Cornerstone Laying Ceremonies Sunday, October 6," *Baltimore Jewish Times*, October 4, 1957.

58 Abba David Poliakoff interview, May 10, 2007, OH 716, JMM.

59 Ibid.

83

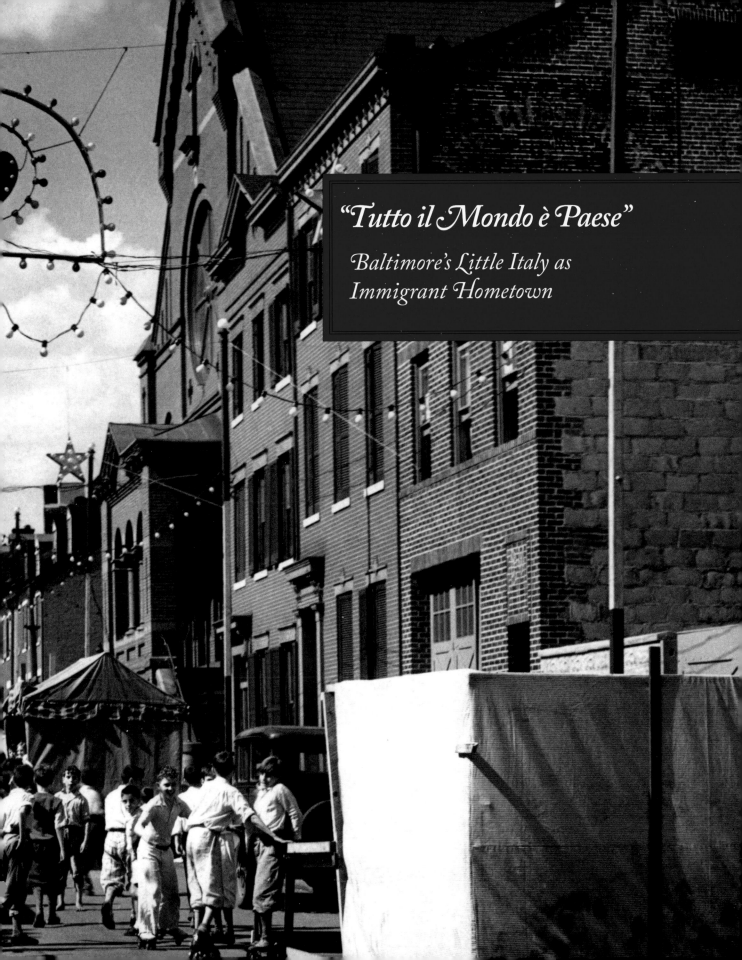

"Tutto il Mondo è Paese"

Baltimore's Little Italy as Immigrant Hometown

"Tutto il Mondo è Paese": Baltimore's Little Italy as Immigrant Hometown

BY MELISSA MARTENS

Melissa Martens is Curator at the Jane Addams Hull-House Museum.

OVERLEAF: *A street festival in Little Italy, 1936. St. Leo's is on the right.*

Photo by A. Aubrey Bodine, copyright Jennifer B. Bodine, courtesy of www.aaubreybodine.com

There is an old Italian saying that goes, "*tutto il mondo è paese*," meaning, "all the world is a small hometown."[1] And without a doubt, the story of the Italian people has been carefully constructed to include their real and folkloric associations with place: they are a people closely identified with their homes, their churches, their burial grounds, their villages, their urban enclaves, their farmlands, their regions, and their native land. In the ongoing Italian cultural narrative—illustrated against this backdrop of "place"—location, itself, is a principal player. It is no surprise, then, that our understanding of the Italians in Baltimore and beyond is inextricably linked to their physical and psychological "hometowns," spaces we know in America as "Little Italies."

In strong contrast to the mythos that the Jews are a disenfranchised people—a people without place, without permanence, without a fixed homeland, a people in exodus, on-the-move, moving up, and moving out—Italians are, perhaps, *over*-identified with their territories. As early as 1866, the first American consul to Venice, William Dean Howells, described the Italians as "a home-loving people" with little tendency toward emigration.[2]

Today, years after Italian mass migration and population growth in the United States, both the peninsula and its American outposts serve as primary links to "Italian-ness," as shown in the imagery of travel posters, postcards, kitsch objects, and the muraled dining rooms of Italian restaurants and social halls. Italians are seen as descendants and defenders of the "turf," with social implications both positive and negative. The Italian-American experience today is viewed in relationship not only to Italy, but also to the Little Italies that survive around America. Baltimore's Little Italy is one of the most vital, a thriving residential neighborhood and tourist destination for suburbanites and out-of-towners. So while the Italian association with land has both authentic and exaggerated dimensions, the cultural weight of this association is undeniable, a key for understanding the neighborhood's evolution.

The staying power of Baltimore's Little Italy is also of particular import for piecing together the story of its East Baltimore surroundings—an area once known best for its overriding Jewish flavor. In recent decades, the popularity and physical articulation of Baltimore's Little Italy have created a new ethnic identity for this neighborhood just east of the Jones Falls. It has survived predictions of economic decline and disappearance into the larger culture, and its celebrated Italian character has now eclipsed all other ethnic associations. As we look at East Baltimore to make sense of its past and its present, what are the cues we can take from these former immigrant streets? What does the area's current configuration tell us about the trajectory of becoming American in Baltimore? How did this neighborhood serve as a place for Italians and Jews to define the "boundaries" of their identities? And, how is the collective ethnic past relived, revived, and renegotiated through the neighborhood today?

A close reading of the "Jewish" and "Italian" blocks of East Baltimore both

Fawn Street, Little Italy, circa 1940.

Photo by A. Aubrey Bodine, copyright Jennifer B.
Bodine, courtesy of www.aaubreybodine.com

confirms and complicates our understanding of the meanings at play. And while stereotypes of Jewish and Italian relationships to the land certainly lend a poetic tone to the historical narratives of both groups, they have often been recited in ways that oversimplify our understanding of neighbors and neighborhood, conveniently assigning causality to complicated historical dynamics. While there are sound reasons to explore the conventional narratives, the ways in which these groups actually navigated and renegotiated the landscapes to which they laid claim complicate our understanding of Baltimore's immigrant hub. If "all the world is a small hometown" in the rubric of Italian culture, then it is essential to contemplate how newcomers to America erected their own pillars of community within the Monumental City.

CREATING AN ITALIAN SQUARE IN THE "GHETTO"

In many ways, the forces that brought Italians in and out of America were set in motion by issues of "home" and "land." Regardless of the people's reputation and self-proclaimed love for their homeland, political and economic tensions

The Schiavo family outside their grocery store in Little Italy.

Courtesy of The Maryland Historical Society

fueled an exodus out of the *Mezzogiorno* after the unification of Italy in the 1860s, when conflicts erupted between the new regime and those who lived in the regions below Rome.[3] In southern Italy and in Sicily, in particular, epidemics, earthquakes, drought, poverty, and tensions between government and workers drove large waves of Italians out of their homeland. By the end of the 1870s, more than 100,000 people were departing annually for other lands, many of them artisans, farmers, and field workers who could no longer tolerate the state's hand in the local agricultural system.[4] One popular Italian song of the era demonstrated the animosity of farm workers toward the rich who remained:

> *Come on, you fine fellows,*
> *throw away your little umbrellas*
> *throw away your gloves*
> *and take our places in the fields.*
> *We are off to America.*[5]

The Italian immigrants who came to America before the 1860s were largely from northern Italy, followed next by southern Italians from Abruzzi, Calabria, Basilicata, and Naples. Baltimore had a small population of Italians from Genoa by the 1870s, enough to warrant a minor reputation for its Italian colony. Many were laborers and peddlers, though some were successful businessmen, including restaurant owner Carlo Rettaliata, confectioner Angelo Baccigalupi, and grocer John Cuneo.[6] But it was the large wave of Sicilians who arrived between the 1880s and 1920s who made the largest impression on America and on Baltimore. During these decades, every fourth immigrant to the United States was from Sicily.[7]

While Baltimore was a major port of entry for Jewish immigrants by the 1880s, it played a much different role in the story of Italian settlement in America. Most Italians came to the ports of New York or Philadelphia and traveled to Baltimore by train, planning to head west in search of work and fortune. Arriving at the railroad station at the base of President Street, a good number sought respite before heading west, and stayed near the station in the lower Jones Falls area.[8] The neighborhood, already home to German, Irish, and native-born families, proved to be a promising locale: Italian laborers found rooms for rent and "pick and ax" work with the railroad and with waterfront industries. By 1880, this trickle of immigrants from southern Italy started to impart a new flavor to the neighborhood, and Italian newcomers began to fill in the blocks between President Street and Central Avenue.

The emerging Italian neighborhood of the 1880s had several important needs to fill before it could sustain a cohesive community. Burials and worship were some of the earliest priorities for the growing colony, as for most newcomers. A plethora of churches and synagogues already served the various ethnic groups who lived or worshiped in the immediate area. St. Vincent de Paul, one of the city's leading Catholic parishes, was a hub for Irish Catholic immigrants. Located along the Jones Falls at Fayette and Front Streets, the church began to attract clusters of Italians by the 1870s.[9]

While St. Vincent's congregants shared a Catholic background, differences in language and traditions created tensions in the house of worship. Italians assembled in the church basement for separate services, though it is unclear if this was by choice. In 1873, the archdiocese hired Rev. Joseph L. Andreis as an assistant pastor to help meet the needs of the growing Italian segment of the parish, as well as clusters of Italians in other churches. Hailing from *northern* Italy, Father Andreis filled a symbolic role as well as an actual one—serving as a suitable representative for all Italian Catholics in Baltimore, yet bringing an elite version of "Italian" into contact with the city's leadership.[10]

In 1879, Archbishop Gibbons asked Father Andreis to report on the Italian population of Baltimore. Andreis responded that there were 500 Italians living in the city, and many more were expected. An 1880 registry for St. Vincent's reveals that approximately 10 percent of the baptisms performed there that year were for Italian families, a marked increase over earlier years.[11] The emerging Italian community no doubt threatened the status of the parish's long-standing, more assimilated members, who had already fought to secure their place in the city. The moment was ripe for the Italians to have a church of their own.

On September 12, 1880, Gibbons laid the cornerstone for Baltimore's first Italian church, St. Leo the Great, a few blocks southeast of St. Vincent's, at Exeter and Stiles Streets. While the decision to create St. Leo's may have been Gibbons's attempt to ease animosity toward the Italians, it created an important foundation on which they could build their community. The procession to celebrate the event was "one of the most imposing demonstrations of its character ever seen in Baltimore," according to *The Mirror*. "The route over which the procession passed was as follows: from South

St. Leo the Great Roman Catholic Church, 2005.

Photo by Carl Caruso, courtesy of Historic Jonestown, Inc.

90

and Baltimore Streets along Baltimore Street to Exeter to Stiles to Central Avenue to Eastern Avenue to High, to Stiles, to Exeter. All along the line the windows of the houses and the sidewalks were thronged with spectators, who thoroughly enjoyed the brilliant spectacle."[12]

St. Leo's was dedicated in 1881, with Father Andreis as its first pastor. While the pastor at St. Vincent's hoped St. Leo's would conduct services only in Italian (thus making it less likely to attract non-Italian Catholics), the new church lacked the resources to continue as an exclusively Italian parish. Local non-Italians constituted the majority of the congregation during its earliest years, though it remained the most comfortable place for Italians to attend services.[13]

St. Leo's would become the backbone of the Italian neighborhood, providing a physical, spiritual, and communal center for Italian life, regardless of participation from congregants of other ethnic backgrounds.[14] The community identity that was forged through church activities solidified the Italian presence in Baltimore by uniting Italians of different dialects, villages, and ideologies, and also by fixing the Italian image for onlookers. Many new Italian immigrants to America practiced an informal version of Catholicism—blending Catholic practices with folk traditions and village customs. The new church for Italians in Baltimore formalized the interpretation of Catholicism for the community and publicly presented Italians as a people of unified practice.

The relationship between Catholicism and community was cemented on the night of February 8, 1904, when the infamous Baltimore Fire ravaged the city's downtown. When the fire began raging eastward from Light Street, advancing with winds up to twenty-five miles per hour, thirty-seven fire engines stationed themselves on the east side of the Jones Falls, bracing themselves and the residents of East Baltimore for the coming flames.[15] A power house exploded nearby, and as one onlooker described it, "Catholics, Protestants and Jews all thought that the end of the world had come. . . . An Italian voice suddenly lifted above all others, 'Saint Anthony, protect us!'" Hundreds of Italians reportedly gathered by the water's edge, bringing a statue of St. Anthony with them from the church.[16]

An anniversary booklet for St. Leo's relates what happened next, according to oral tradition: "The stage was set for a miracle. Many of the parishioners refused to leave their homes and belongings they had worked so hard to earn. Instead, they gathered . . . and prayed to God to spare them from the flames . . . as Fr. Monteverde raised his arms in prayer, they made a solemn vow: if their homes and church were spared from the fire, they would hold a yearly festival in honor of St. Anthony. At about 6 o'clock . . . a strong wind came up and blew the flames the other way."[17]

Differing accounts describe varying levels of participation from the residents, though even the least dramatic rendition cites the role of religion in "saving the neighborhood." One person recalled:

Most of the people had gone to Highlandtown. The few of us left went into Nick Barone's saloon on President Street near Eastern Avenue. . . . We were there for company and comfort. About 11:30 that night old Julius Tosches . . . came in. He was excited. He told us he was running down the street, away from the fire, when St. Anthony came to him. He was in a black robe, and he told him not to be afraid. The saint told him that the fire would not burn Little Italy. Later we went to the church and prayed to St. Anthony. The fire stopped.[18]

Whether it was the wind, the prayers, the position of the Jones Falls, or the wall of water created by the fire hoses, the fire's retreat initiated an appreciation for Little Italy and its citizens. Emphasizing the role of religion and the passionate participation of neighborhood residents, the story (perpetuated by Italians and non-Italians, alike) secured the legitimacy of Little Italy in Baltimore lore. An annual procession and festival in honor of St. Anthony symbolically reenacts the legendary story, creating a psychic link between the Italians and Baltimore's very survival in the face of disaster.

Though the fire helped establish the place of Italians in Baltimore, their adjustment to city life in America was not easy. As for most immigrants, starting life anew was overwhelming financially, logistically, and emotionally. Many who left Italy had few resources and came with skills better suited to rural life: tenant farming, field working, sheepherding, fishing, woodworking, stonecutting, mining, cooking, and baking.[19] Yet most of the concentrated Italian settlements in America were in cities. Compared with immigrant groups who had a more urban experience in their homelands, many Italians were overwhelmed by the new culture and the unfamiliar landscape.

First encounters with America were often frustrating and disappointing. One Italian immigrant recorded his impressions of arrival in New York: "Noise is everywhere, the din is constant and it completely fills my head." Another proclaimed, "The streets are full of horse manure. My town in Italy, Avelino, was much more beautiful. I said to myself, 'How come, America?'" While not all who came through New York planned to settle there, it represented the Immigrant City and the New World—a world that stood in stark contrast to the pastures and vineyards of Italy.[20]

Coming to America was not necessarily a permanent situation for all Italians who made the journey. Some came with plans to return when economic conditions improved in Italy, saving newly earned money to send or take back home. Others came in stages, the man of the household arriving first to evaluate prospects for living in America. Voyages back to the *Mezzogiorno* were common and frequent, whether to find a wife, reestablish ties, persuade family members to move abroad, or resettle in Italy. Approximately half of those who returned to Italy decided to stay there.[21]

Many others, such as Ida Esposito's grandfather, decided to remain in Baltimore after much deliberation. "He was very excited because he had heard so much about America," she states. "But he decided just to come over so that he could add an addition of one room to his home in Abruzzi, Italy. And he stayed here for about three years and he went back. Then he decided, 'Italy is not for me anymore; I'm going back to America.' It was easier living, he said. He brought his son over with him."[22]

For those who decided to stay in America, creating an Italian-style village in the city had tremendous emotional and cultural import. Early arrivals set the tone, creating an environment that encouraged Italian celebrations, language, foodways, and traditions in order to attract family or friends. While Baltimore's scenery hardly resembled that of an Italian village, newcomers sought to reenact the lifestyles of their homeland in their new surrounds. For many, this meant participating in outdoor activities, such as urban gardening and socializing in the streets. Outdoor gatherings large and small would remain a hallmark of community life. Ida Esposito remembers impromptu card games taking place on the sidewalks during the Depression, an activity that brought neighborhood residents together in difficult times.[23]

The streets themselves provided the principal stage for performing iden-

A parade in Little Italy.
Courtesy of The Maryland Historical Society

tity, as the setting where immigrants learned what it meant to be American and ethnic at the same time. Many Italians saw their experiences on the streets as central to their communal and personal identities. As Richard Chiapparelli put it, "I was raised on these streets; when I marry I would prefer to marry an Italian girl who was raised on these streets too." The streets demarcated a sense of place that became so strong that it sometimes overrode ethnic identification. One of Frank Verde's uncles was so disappointed to learn that his daughter was marrying someone from another part of town that he proclaimed, "Why don't you just marry someone from the neighborhood, like a nice Jewish boy."[24]

Little Italy developed a distinctive look owing to its outdoor life, one that still distinguishes it today. The landscape reflected the communal pride of a people with strong traditions in farming and the building trades. Defining features included festive streetlights, bocce courts, processions, plantings, manicured exteriors, and window decorations. One Jewish man who grew up nearby remembers that the shift from the Jewish to Italian neighborhood was most clearly marked by statuettes of saints that decorated the windows of Italian homes. Yet, despite the existence of a geographic district clearly distinguishable as Italian in character, much of the territory was negotiable and overlapped with the surrounding neighborhood, creating a place in which Jews and Italians could negotiate their similarities and differences.

DEFINING AND SHARING THE TURF

The domain that became known as Baltimore's Little Italy was described as early as 1881 in the aforementioned account of the parade for St. Leo's opening day: Exeter Street, Stiles, High, Central, and Eastern Avenue constituted the backbone of the procession's route. The generally agreed-upon boundaries of Little Italy have been relatively fixed for around one hundred years: Pratt Street to the north, Eastern Avenue to the south, Central Avenue to the east, and President Street to the west (see map on inside front cover).

From the 1890s to the 1930s, the city's primary Jewish immigrant neighborhood flourished directly to the north, above Pratt Street. Aaron Smelkinson, who grew up on Central Avenue in the 1910s, perceived the division between the Jewish and the Italian neighborhoods as quite rigid. "Little Italy was there, but there was a dividing line as if it was a wire fence. . . . You got beat up if you got past Pratt Street." Other oral histories echo his account of boys defending their turf based on ethnic identification.[25]

Yet, Little Italy's boundaries have been more permeable than such memories suggest, both demographically and culturally. At the turn of the twentieth century, the "Italian district" was quite diverse—in fact, more Jews lived there than Italians.[26] They established numerous synagogues on or below Pratt Street, some of which continued to flourish even after the neighborhood became heavily Italian in the 1910s. These included Adas Jeshurun (840 East Pratt,

1890-1912), Agudas Achim Anshe Chernigov (1107 East Pratt before 1916), Anshe Bobruisk Nusach Ari (1104 East Pratt before 1916), and Shomrei Hadath (1010 East Pratt, 1896-1930). One of East Baltimore's largest synagogues, Beth Hamedrosh Hagodol, operated in the heart of Little Italy on High and Stiles Street from 1899 to 1935.[27]

Nor were Italians confined to Little Italy. Many lived north of Pratt Street even during the years when the area was considered a Jewish immigrant ghetto. When Jews began to move away in the 1920s and 1930s, the area became more Italian than Jewish. Some Italian residents recall the boundaries of "their" territory as extending as far north as Belair Market and also reaching south and east into Fells Point.[28]

While attitudes and cultural cues reinforced distinctions between the Italian and Jewish districts, many felt comfortable crossing or stretching boundaries for socializing, sports, shopping, and other activities. Some former residents recall tensions between Jewish and Italian street gangs, while others emphasize how the streets created opportunities for spontaneous interaction. Louis Schwartz, who grew up on Baltimore Street, recalled that "almost every Italian family would get in a shipment of grapes from the truck because

TOP: *The Sun of Italy Food Products warehouse at the corner of Stiles and Albemarle Streets, 1989. The building housed Congregation Beth Hamedrosh Hagodol Agudas Achim from 1899 to 1935.*

Gift of Marvin Diamond, JMM 1989.106.11

BOTTOM: *Interior of the Sun of Italy Food Products warehouse, showing ornamentation from when the building housed the Beth Hamedrosh congregation.*

Photo by Aaron Levin, JMM 1991.89.7

they made their own wine. We used to hang around and try to grab the loose grapes that fell off the truck." Family events became neighborhood events, he continued. "I remember a big Italian wedding; the whole neighborhood took part in it. They had these candy-coated almonds and were throwing them out to everybody, and the kids were grabbing them." Schwartz's father even participated in church activities, playing horn in the St. Gabriel's procession and later joining the Our Lady of Pompeii band in Highlandtown.[29]

The proximity of Italians to their Jewish neighbors across Pratt Street led many Italian children to serve in the capacity of *shabbos goy*, performing small tasks that Jewish law forbids Jews to do on the Sabbath. Joseph Sergi was one of them. "We played together. Then on a Saturday is where I made my nickels and dimes. . . . Jewish kids couldn't light the stoves on the Sabbath so they used to leave two or three cents up on the mantelpiece. Every time I'd light the stove there, you know, it got nice and warm." Such interactions underscore the growing respect between the two groups. Clara Rizzi Ferretti remembers cultivating her reputation as a reliable *shabbos goy*. "On Friday nights and Saturday mornings, we would go turn the gas on . . . they wouldn't call everybody, just the ones they trusted."[30]

One of the many reasons Italians and Jews lived rather comfortably side-by-side was their shared sense of otherness. Newcomers had much to prove to gain approval, status, and better treatment from public officials and more established groups. Italians had further to go than most immigrants: according to a 1910 study by the U.S. Immigration Commission, they were the lowest income earners in the country besides African Americans.[31] Southern Italians, who were generally seen as inferiors by their countrymen in Italy, enjoyed no improved status upon their arrival in America. Like Eastern European Jews, who bore the brunt of American anxieties about the vast hordes of immigrants who arrived between 1880 and 1924, southern Italians occupied a low position on the black/white continuum. Some social observers, including Dutch-American journalist Jacob Riis, argued that Italians and Jews were inferior to the "Negro" in matters such as cleanliness, therefore making them undesirable tenants and, by extension, citizens.[32]

Fitting in, yet still maintaining one's distinctiveness, was a tricky process. While some efforts to Americanize were instinctual behaviors on the part of immigrants—learning English, trying new foods, dressing in American clothing—others were initiated by social reformers, philanthropists, and city officials. Such social experiments included settlement houses, tenement legislation, public parks, and sanitary reform.[33]

One of the more successful strategies for improving Baltimore's "slums" was the bathhouse movement. The establishment of public baths satisfied the city's civic-minded leaders, invested immigrants with personal pride, and strengthened relations between neighbors. The need for public baths in the immigrant section of East Baltimore was compelling: after Philadelphia, Baltimore had more people per household than any other American city. In

96

Inside the men's section of the Walters Public Baths.
Courtesy of Jacques Kelly

Walters Public Bath, 131 South High Street, 1900.
Courtesy of The Maryland Historical Society

an 1893 investigation of Baltimore's most crowded slum districts, the Federal
Bureau of Labor revealed that less than 8 percent of families had bathrooms
in their homes or tenements.[34] Households often lacked hot water and
many had no indoor plumbing at all. Under such conditions, bathing was an
arduous process, and both Jews and Italians who grew up in East Baltimore
recall the preparations required for Friday night Sabbath or Sunday mass,
including thorough bathing and dressing in fine clothes.

Social reformers launched Baltimore's Bath Commission in 1894, and
a few years later they interested railroad magnate and art collector Henry
Walters in their cause. In February of 1899, Walters stated that he was
"willing to erect three baths in Baltimore at a cost not exceeding $15,000
each, the baths to be known as the Walters Public Baths." Walters later
explained that "in the poorer sections of Baltimore, especially in the neighborhoods where the foreign people dwelt, there was room for great improvement
in sanitary conditions. When you consider that in some houses from 100 to
150 people are congregated without means for keeping clean you can realize,
as I did, what a boon a public bath house would be."[35]

The movement to create bathhouses in Baltimore expressed the city's
desire to cleanse the "unwashed" masses both physically and metaphori-

'I CAME OUT BEAUTY WHITE'

This cartoon appeared in the Baltimore Evening Sun *on June 7, 1951.*

cally, and to provide a mechanism for uplift. By teaching middle class values through public washing, bathhouses tried to infuse a sense of stability and unity in the slums.[36] The act of cleansing provided a new image for immigrant communities—one of reform, rehabilitation, acceptance of middle-class norms, and a literal wiping away of past hardships. A cartoon that appeared in a newspaper decades later depicted a man combing his hair after a shower at the free baths; the caption below states, "I Came Out Beauty White."[37] While punning on the brand of soap used at the bath house, the cartoon also implies the transformative powers assigned to the act of becoming physically clean.

Intentions aside, the local bathhouse proved to be one of the most likely places for Jews and Italians to mingle in the neighborhood. The city's first and most legendary bathhouse opened on May 18, 1900. Walters Bath No. 1 was located at 131 South High Street, midway between the Italian and Jewish districts. While there were eventually other city bathhouses, the one on High Street was the most popular and beloved.[38] Equipped with eighteen showers for men, five showers and two tubs for women, and a public laundry for itinerants, the bathhouse served 48,827 people in its first year and 250,672 during its peak in 1914. By the time Bath No. 1 closed its doors in 1954, it had served some 8.7 million bathers, many of whom were Jewish and Italian.[39] Going to the baths was more than an opportunity for cleanliness; it provided personal satisfaction and uplift. As one Jewish user put it: "I wanted to go to the bathhouse because it was a very social thing to do." An Italian woman even proclaimed, "Going to the bathhouse, I thought I was in Hollywood."[40]

A sold-out reunion attracting hundreds of Jews and Italians to the Sons of Italy Lodge in 1996 was a testament to the deep communal meanings associated with the neighborhood bathhouse, as well the fondness that developed between the two groups through this shared experience. Reunion attendees ate pasta together, socialized, danced to "Havah Negilah," and reminisced at the microphone. Paul Wartzman reflected on the bathhouse as shared space. "There will never [again] be a situation where Jewish men and women and Italian men and women take baths under the same roof."[41]

Many of the core essentials of life—shopping, eating, and bathing—were made more pleasurable and palatable with neighborly cooperation and participation. The very simplicity of such daily routines created a sense of "being all-in-it-together"—an empathy between those striving to create a better life. The camaraderie between the two groups was apparent in the remarks by Clara Rizzo Ferretti at the 1996 reunion. "I'd love to welcome you here, all of our beautiful Jewish neighbors and friends. I lived on Lombard Street, four or five Italian families," she told the crowd. "I was always proud to have grown up in the Jewish neighborhood . . . . 'Once a Lombard Street girl, always a Lombard Street girl.'"[42]

Lombard Street may have been the main thoroughfare of the Jewish neighborhood, yet shopping on Lombard Street also taught others how to navigate ethnicity and assimilation within a narrative of upward mobility.

Jewish businesses served as daily reminders of the story of immigrant progress, especially to those who saw themselves on a similar socioeconomic trajectory.[43] Establishments such as Attman's and Tulkoff's celebrated the Old World and permitted outsiders of all kinds to relish in the delights of distinctiveness. Delicatessens, in particular, directly referenced the struggles of the past, serving pickled and salted foods coming out of the recipes of poverty. Yet with their bustling business and successful proprietors, delis simultaneously reminded customers just how far this immigrant group had come in the New World. By pointing simultaneously to both struggle and success, Jews served as a model for other striving groups.

Lombard Street stores such as Pastore's and Garofalo's operated side by side with Jewish businesses, forging long-standing friendships and commercial relationships. First and foremost, businesses aimed to serve shoppers from their own background, as Shirley Yacobani describes. "Now honestly, the Jewish stores had the majority of the Jewish trade. We being Italian, we had the majority of the Italian trade. . . . But if one or the other ran out of something, they wouldn't hesitate to go to the other. . . . Because my parents were in business, I got to know all the family businesses that were Jewish."[44]

While catering primarily to their own cultural group, neither community could operate in isolation from its neighbors. Both Jewish and Italian retailers relied heavily on a diverse customer base. Lucy Vecera's family shopped on Lombard Street regularly. She recalled, "My uncle Tom would come down to Lombard Street and buy a kid goat for Easter, and have it butchered. Of course they were butchering it in kosher style!" Jews also made use of Italian foods and services. First encounters with Italian foods were not always convincing. As Louis Schwartz recalled of his early memories of Lordi's grocery store, "I didn't like to go in there because it smelled so bad because it basically was an Italian store. And I couldn't stand the smell of those cheeses and all that they had hanging around."[45]

Nonetheless, Jews were some of the first American residents to sample new cuisines such as Italian restaurant foods. Advertisements for Italian restaurants were common in the local Jewish press in the early twentieth century, and many food businesses in Little Italy benefited from frequent Jewish patronage. In 1936, for example, an article in Baltimore's *Jewish Times* titled "Italian Villa Scores Hit with the Patrons" reported that Marina Cavaliere Allori opened her own business on 300 South Albemarle Street, since her cooking at another neighborhood establishment had proven popular and had "gained a large Jewish following."[46]

Melding the language, religion, and traditions from many cultures, this neighborhood of newcomers was a ground for experimenting in the ways of America. With so many sharing the neighborhood's space and history, East Baltimore became a place to assert one's identity, refine or recast one's values, and negotiate one's standing in the world as both an "ethnic" and an "American." As the variation in definitions of "Jewish" and "Italian" bound-

The 1000 block of East Lombard Street, 1969.
Photo by A. Aubrey Bodine, copyright Jennifer B. Bodine, courtesy of www.aaubreybodine.com

99

A DiGiorgio Fruit Company delivery truck.
Courtesy of The Maryland Historical Society

aries suggests, these ethnic neighborhoods were both fixed and fluid spaces. Both groups created distinct areas that announced their resistance to the New World, yet fostered cooperation and the cross-pollination of cultures. Newcomers in a strange land, Jews and Italians learned to live side by side while staking their own claims to America.

THE ENDURING VILLAGE: LITTLE ITALY TODAY

In many other towns, the various Little Italys . . . are shrinking, giving way to trendier restaurants, new waves of immigrants, and rising real estate costs. But our Little Italy is, in many ways, same as it ever was . . . only better.

Baltimore Magazine, July 2005

American cities today make much of their "ethnic" neighborhoods—the Greektowns, Little Koreas, Chinatowns, and Los Barrios that appear as colorful zones on slick maps and in tourist guides. As pointers to the past and signifiers of the reborn American city, ethnic enclaves serve many functions. They generate tourism, create economic stability, infuse cities with a sense of peoplehood, and construct urban narrative. They encourage ethnic differentiation, foreground multiculturalism, and celebrate cultures—albeit in ways simplified for the mainstream. Yet despite the recent rebirth of such enclaves in many cities, Baltimore has relatively few neighborhoods that convey a sense of coherent cultural identity.

By far the most identifiable ethnic-themed neighborhood in Baltimore today is its Little Italy. And while the survival of a Little Italy is not a unique occurrence, its uninterrupted lifespan, relatively undisturbed location, stable residential population, and contemporary vitality are notable—particularly when compared to other Italian districts in America and other ethnic neighborhoods around Baltimore.[47] As early as 1969, an article in the *Baltimore Sun* made note of Little Italy's remarkable staying power: "Other ethnic communities have greatly shrunk, moved on, or have disappeared altogether; but you will find that Little Italy is today block for block where it was fifty years ago, and just about the same size."[48]

In contrast to Baltimore's other downtown neighborhoods—many of which are now heavily developed or in transition—Little Italy remains a stable urban village with all the visible signs of its ethnic past. The markers of the neighborhood relay a sense of tradition and continuity, including its well-maintained formstone homes, marble steps, Italian flags, banners, year-round Christmas lights, and bold restaurant signs announcing "Vellegia's," "DaMimmo's," and "Cesar's Den." Like an Italian Brigadoon in the midst of urbania, the neighborhood's features conjure the bygone Old World. As a resident once put it, "I love these blocks so much, that I would like to build a fence around them, to keep them like this—Italian—forever!"[49]

While the staying power of Baltimore's Little Italy today seems inevi-

table, profound questions challenged the Italian "place" in American society throughout the twentieth century—literally, physically, poetically, and metaphorically. Italian newcomers faced the dilemma of choosing a primary identity—Italian or American. And while many maintained their love for Italy despite their decision to stay in America, their affection for their homeland would take different forms as the decades passed. Ultimately, the Italian-American appreciation for and association with land would shift loci, from Italy to America.

After the decision to return to Italy or stay in America, devotion to the homeland was next tested by international affairs. By 1922, Mussolini's rise to power created a new image for Italy. Quite a few Italian Americans initially supported the early version of the regime (as did some other Americans), and many felt pride in Italy's new, ascending leadership. Lingering memories of problems in the motherland left Italian émigrés craving a stronger, more powerful country of origin. Furthermore, as victims of discrimination in America, Italian Americans welcomed the opportunity for national pride and the chance to redeem their reputation on the international stage.

Yet, by the time Mussolini entered his "Pact of Steel" with Hitler in

Lopresti's Grocery on Stiles Street in Little Italy.
JMM CP11.2007.2

South Exeter Street in Little Italy, 1936.

Courtesy of the Library of Congress, Prints &
Photographs Division

1939, Italian-American support of *Il Duce* had waned. And when the United
States entered World War II in 1941, Italian Americans firmly supported
the Allied cause. [50] In Baltimore, enthusiasm for the war effort was palpable,
as demonstrated by a flag dedication in the square at Eastern Avenue and
High Street. More than 1,000 neighbors cheered as a large flag adorned with
eighty-five blue stars was raised, each star representing an enlisted soldier
from Little Italy. Congressman Tommy D'Alesandro, Jr., addressed the crowd
that day, exclaiming, "Away with Hitler! Away with Mussolini! Away with the
Japanese!"[51]

Substantial participation in the armed forces during World War II
helped Italian Americans to secure a seat at the American table, as was also
the case for Jewish Americans. But the reality of being both American and
Italian was not always easy, for America was pitted very firmly against Italy

in the conflict, and Italian Americans came under a cloud of suspicion.[52] The connection between Italians and their lands—always a defining feature of their culture—was particularly problematic during the war years.

A decade after the war ended, the construction of the Flag House Courts public housing development provoked a new set of complex attitudes regarding Italian "boundaries" in Baltimore. Shared territories and frequent contact between minorities had previously created alliances throughout the larger neighborhood, with fluid boundaries and relatively few intra-group tensions. But by the 1950s, the dynamics would shift profoundly.

When a major chunk of the formerly Jewish neighborhood north of Little Italy was cleared in 1953 to make room for the new public housing complex, it affected Italians both north and south of Pratt Street. The demolition changed the visual texture of the neighborhood immediately, removing a huge number of rowhouses that defined East Baltimore and replacing them with blocks of modern apartment buildings, including three massive high rises. Of the families displaced by this "slum clearance," 65 percent were white, many Italian.[53] They relocated to temporary quarters, or moved deeper into Little Italy or further away from the city's core. The displacement had a profound impact on the way Little Italy's residents saw their neighborhood—for the blocks on both sides of Pratt were no longer defined only by mood, décor, and residential concentrations. The physical change in the landscape created a visible dividing line between the old and the new, the subsidized and the non-subsidized.

When Flag House Courts first opened in 1955, at least 60 percent of its housing units were occupied by white families, and relations among the various groups were initially hospitable. Italians were among the first families to move into Flag House Courts, yet they did not stay for long. By 1970, only 3 percent of the residents in the complex were white. This shift reflected urban trends across American cities. As increased opportunities enabled working-class whites to improve their economic status and achieve the American dream of homeownership, low-income neighborhoods (including public housing) became disproportionately African American. Racial tensions rose between whites who were anxious to protect their new status and blacks who were frustrated and angry about their continued lack of opportunity.[54] Italians who chose to remain in Little Italy rather than follow their compatriots into the suburbs felt increasingly beleaguered.

The unrest of the late 1960s hardened the social and actual boundaries between groups. When the riots that followed Martin Luther King, Jr.'s, assassination hit Lombard Street on April 7, 1968, both Jewish- and Italian-owned businesses were in the path of the chaos. The *Baltimore Sun* commented, "the only stores that were not damaged were Jack's Delicatessen and Little Italy, where the owners stayed in the store during the recent disorder and protected them with weapons."[55] In fact, Lombard Street suffered relatively minor damage aside from a couple of hard-hit stores, but

103

the image of Italian storeowners protecting their businesses became part of Little Italy's legend. The riots had both a disruptive and solidifying effect on the Italian community. They calcified the communal instinct to preserve the neighborhood, as had been the case after the 1904 Fire, and as would be the case when highway proposals threatened to demolish historic neighborhoods in the city's core in 1969. [56]

By the 1970s, the area north of Pratt Street became known more for its poverty and crime than for its immigrant past. Residents of Little Italy who might have once proudly seen themselves as part of the continuum of varied newcomers and strivers in a loosely defined immigrant center now stood on one side of a dividing line that separated black from white, poor from middle class. One 1974 article observed, "once the neighborhood became Italian, it stayed Italian; and should one family move, the house sells quickly to another by word of mouth."[57] The goal of maintaining a cohesive Italian neighborhood was driven mostly by instincts of community pride, yet it might also have reflected a desire to exclude. Little Italy had become one of the most distinctive all-white neighborhoods in the center of a city divided.

Even though most downtown neighborhoods declined rapidly in the 1970s and 1980s, some trends in those same years actually increased Little Italy's chance at survival. The general acceptance of Italians and their elevated social standing helped generate a national and local appreciation for Italian food, art, and culture. Many ethnic groups in America who were initially insecure about their status began celebrating their heritage. One 1975 newspaper article about Little Italy even proclaimed, "Ethnicity is Coming Back as the 'In' Thing."[58] Alex Haley's 1976 novel *Roots* stimulated mass interest in genealogy, while affordable air travel helped Americans reconnect with their geographic and cultural origins. So while urban living in Baltimore had become decidedly unfashionable by these decades, "Italian-ness" in America had reached new levels of popularity—for both insiders and outsiders.

Popular culture was an important arena in which Italian Americans became noticed, from Frank Sinatra to Hollywood films. But the complicated images of Italian Americans generated through the movies stimulated both fear and intrigue in the public imagination. Blockbusters featuring Italian Americans—*The Godfather, Mean Streets, Rocky,* and *Saturday Night Fever*—did not necessarily flatter Italian Americans, but they did strongly reconnect them to the notions of neighborhood, turf, and the streets.

Not only did such films show Italian Americans as protectors of their urban territories, but some even wove cautionary tales about the disadvantages of suburbia. In *The Godfather, Part II*, for example, Vito Corleone struggles to maintain power in his old Manhattan neighborhood while living in isolation in a Long Island mansion. This theme would later surface in the HBO series *The Sopranos*—the show's well-known opening portrays Tony Soprano driving from Manhattan through the Lincoln Tunnel, past the industrial Meadowlands, through the old Italian district of Newark, and into his

A Little Italy street scene.
JMM CP11.2007.4

cul-de-sac home in the suburbs where he must try to reconcile old-world problems with new ones. The very act of leaving Little Italy has often been portrayed as a painful and regrettable experience.[59]

In his 1974 book on Baltimore's Little Italy, journalist Gilbert Sandler noted the ambivalence Italian Americans felt toward suburbia. He quoted Isidore Travoato, who moved back to "The Neighborhood" in the 1970s. "I used to live way out in Dundalk, but . . . . we got lonely out there. We wanted to hear Italian spoken again; we wanted the life of Little Italy. So, we moved back!"[60]

Staying or reuniting with the neighborhood not only afforded the conveniences of the nearby church, the Sons of Italy Lodge, community activities, and the popular restaurants, but also provided status to residents as guardians of the old way of life. Maintaining an Italian town square within Baltimore became an impulse that was more than personal—it was communal. Organizations such as the Little Italy Community Association and the Little Italy Restaurant Association created community-driven approaches to maintaining Italian identity in the neighborhood. The self-conscious preservation of Italian-ness affixed to a certain square of blocks became a part of the ongoing relationship of Italians to the hometown they had created.

Perhaps the least expected variable in the neighborhood's survival was the revived popularity of church services at St. Leo's beginning around 1998. As the century came to a close, Catholicism in America was filled with uncertainty and doubt: attendance at churches was dropping, scandal was in the national news, and the fastest growing Catholic population consisted of religiously conservative Hispanic immigrants who, just like the Italians one hundred years earlier, brought with them new languages and traditions that

seemed foreign to established Catholic parishes.

St. Leo's was facing its own particular challenges at the close of the century: regular Sunday masses typically attracted only 200 congregants or fewer, the Italian-language mass had even poorer attendance, the school had been converted into an adult learning center that was new and struggling, and the church had no parking lot.[61] These predicaments were induced and worsened by ongoing suburbanization as well as the aging of the elderly population that comprised the core of the Catholic community in the immediate neighborhood.

Following the passing of the beloved Father Pandola in 1997, Father Michael Louis Salerno arrived from New York City to lead the congregation. He infused St. Leo's with new energy from the very start, as one memoir recounts:

> *Sunday, June 14, 1998. At 9:30 Mass, the church is packed. Close to 500 are in attendance. . . . Fr. Mike Salerno, the new Pallotine Order pastor from "Hell's Kitchen" in the "Big Apple" is already in gear. A dead ringer for a "mussed up Jerry Colonna," Fr. Mike delivers a serious message with a humorous ring, an Italian trait. Loud, soft, effusive and sad, he talks of the meaning of community. Of how sticking together and helping one another is not an outgrown myth. Of how Italians in this community continue to help each other make it.[62]*

Within a few years, Father Mike had secured parking for congregants in a nearby parking lot, the adult learning center was thriving, new relationships between the church and the neighborhood's restaurants had been strengthened, and attendance at Sunday mass was averaging 700.[63] Father Mike himself estimated that of the approximate 1,100 residents in Little Italy in 2005, about 1,000 were Catholic, and that about 30 percent of his congregants were Italians from the neighborhood. The rest came from Towson, Timonium, Perry Hall, and Canton—new congregants as well as those returning to the neighborhood for services. Of the total number of congregants, Father Mike estimated about 60 percent to be Italian.[64]

Like Father Richard Lawrence, the long-standing charismatic leader of St. Vincent de Paul's, Father Mike serves as spiritual leader for the new era, a neighborhood activist, a bridge between cultures, and a figure capable of navigating the complicated role of Catholicism in today's communities. Moreover, Father Mike serves as a walking, breathing link between the Old World and the New: from immigrant culture to American culture, from New York to Baltimore, from young to old, from former street kid to community leader. Today he can frequently be found walking the streets of Little Italy, chatting with passersby and patronizing the local businesses. As Sergi Vitale, co-owner of Aldo's restaurant recently remarked, "He's perfect for Little Italy. It's such a raucous community, such a divided community, that only he can bring it together. He's talking the word of God, but he's walking the streets in

OPPOSITE: The Old Gas Light, *Little Italy, 1957.*

Photo by Thomas Scilipoti, courtesy of Thomas Scilipoti

a T-shirt smoking a cigar. . . . He's a rock star in the neighborhood. He comes by the film festival and everybody knows him. He's Bono."[65]

The revival of St. Leo's Church as a lively spiritual and neighborhood center crystallized the community's core values. Meanwhile, as the neighborhood entered the new century, Baltimore was positioned for a real estate boom, and most of the neighborhoods along the water's edge escalated dramatically in value, including Little Italy. Career-minded young adults from around the East Coast moved into the city in great numbers, and empty nesters in the suburbs discovered a new brand of urban life near downtown Baltimore, filled with energy and new entertainment options. When Flag House Courts was torn down in 2001 to make way for mixed-income townhouses, Little Italy was positioned for dramatic rebirth.

The Little Italy Open Air Film Festival, founded in 1999 to make use of a wooden canvas placed on a building exterior for an ill-fated welcome sign, ushered in a new reason to celebrate in the streets of Little Italy. When John Pente volunteered his third-floor bedroom window as a projection room, a new tradition was born. On pleasant summer nights, more than 800 people can now be found on lawn chairs in the parking lot at the corner of High and Stiles Streets—sampling take-out foods from nearby restaurants, drinking wine, and gazing up to the screen and the sky. Many of the films and viewers are Italian American, but the increasingly diverse audience also enjoys films such as *Avalon*, *Life is Beautiful*, and *My Big, Fat Greek Wedding* as well as *Moonstruck*, *Rocky*, and *Roman Holiday*. Sometimes a reporter from the *New York Times* is even watching from the sidelines in awe of the little Little Italy that made it big. It is a living, breathing *Cinema Paradiso*. [66]

Along with many other representations of Italian culture, Little Italy stands as a reminder that ethnic differentiation can endure, and even be celebrated. Italian culture today cues images of red sauce, bocce matches, trips to Italy, and gourmet gelato. Even the dark *Sopranos* series generated a new lingo appropriated by many Americans who wanted to shout "Bada Bing" and "Fughetaboutit" to the world.

Perhaps much of America is willing to play the crypto-Italian from time to time. Standing in for both the new immigrant and the old, for those who made it and those who are striving, for those who are pale-skinned and those who are dark, Italian Americans enjoy a place in society that speaks to authenticity, yet from a safe distance. Little Italy serves as the archetypal immigrant playground for both insiders and outsiders, providing an encounter with the "safe danger" that Americans seek from the Italian-American pop narrative.[67] Serving as a stage set that permits one to be just a little bit different and a little more ethnic, the Italian town square in Baltimore reminds all who come that they have both arrived and are still ascending.

EPILOGUE: THOSE WHO CAME, AND THOSE WHO STAYED

Strangely, there is no exact word for "home" in the Italian language. Italians speak more precisely of their *casa*, their *famiglia*, their *fucolaro*, their *paesani*, and the *paese*.[68] For a people so tied to the land, perhaps the concept of home was always meant to be somewhat poetic, fluid, and shared. The sixteen or so blocks of Baltimore that have been known as an Italian neighborhood for more than a hundred years are both real and perceived, frozen and forming, Italian and public.

The Little Italy Film Festival.

Courtesy of the Baltimore Area Convention and Visitors Association

There is something undeniably reassuring about the staying power of Little Italy. While plans for Harbor East and the partly subsidized new Albemarle Square town homes change the texture of the area almost daily, Little Italy offers familiarity and reassurance. There one can encounter the past, taste traditions, view the immigrant image in film, gather for worship, and speak Italian to more than a few passersby on the streets. Little Italy holds up so well because it functions as both reality and mirror. Just a few blocks away on Lombard Street, Attman's Delicatessen does much the same for Jewish and non-Jewish customers—do all patrons know what a "Kibbitz Room" is? Probably not, but they go anyway, and they kibbitz, and the space functions as a town square for a certain type of "Jewish-ness."

Yet the disappearance of Jewish life and the perseverance of Italian life in the area are unmistakable characteristics of the space. Conventional explanations for this difference sound as simple as: "Jews moved up quickly," "Italians were not as upwardly mobile," "Jews lacked an attachment to the land," "Italians cared too much about land." As is usual with stereotypes, there are kernels of truth here, but these "explanations" oversimplify a complex cultural process. Both groups planned to move to greener pastures, and both did—though at different times. Both groups retained something "urban" in their identities, though in very different ways. And both retained the immigrant arrival story in their personal and communal narratives, though in different formats. The similarities are there, but the geographic differences overshadow the subtleties.

Why the heart of Italian life still beats in East Baltimore speaks to a number of variables intentional and coincidental: ties to St. Leo's Church and to the homes Italians made there, the intergenerational occupancy of households, the fact that the Baltimore Fire stopped a block away from the neighborhood, the endurance of street celebrations, outdoor decorations, the success of the restaurants, the growing popularity of Italian culture, the arrival of Father Mike, and the fact that John Pente's third floor window was available for projecting movies onto a parking lot wall. Neighborhoods survive or disappear for many such reasons.

Yet the search for "home" is one that is ongoing for all groups, everywhere. In Jewish culture, Israel answers that question, in part, for now. For Italians, perhaps home could be anywhere, "*tutto il mondo è paese.*"

110

NOTES

My sincere thanks are extended for the research assistance provided by Frank Verde and the Church of St. Leo the Great. Thanks also to my parents, and my dear friends Kimry Perrone, Peter Constable, Erik Monti, and Holly Tominack—who taught me quite a bit about enjoying the delights of Little Italy.

1   Translation originally observed by author in exhibition text for "Home & Beast" at the American Visionary Art Museum in Baltimore. See http://www.avam.org/exhibitions/index.html for sample usage of this common phrase.

2   Jerre Mangione and Ben Morreale, *La Storia: Five Centuries of the Italian American Experience* (New York: Harper Collins Publishers, 1992), 67.

3   The *Mezzogiorno* refers to southern Italy, including the islands of Sicily and Sardinia. Historically, the region was economically underdeveloped compared to central and northern Italy.

4   Mangione and Morreale, *La Storia*, 69-72.

5   Ibid., 72.

6   Thomas W. Spalding and Kathryn M. Kuranda,

St. Vincent De Paul of Baltimore: The Story of a People and Their Home (Baltimore: Maryland Historical Society, 1995), 88.

7   Mangione and Morreale, *La Storia*, 78.

8   Gilbert Sandler, *The Neighborhood: The Story of Baltimore's Little Italy* (Baltimore: Bodine & Associates, Inc., 1974), 23.

9   Spalding and Kuranda, *St. Vincent De Paul of Baltimore*, 88.

10   Ibid., 88-89. Other churches with Italian contingents were St. Joseph's and St. Patrick's.

11   Ibid.

12   Quoted in Sandler, *The Neighborhood*, 26.

13   Spalding and Kuranda, *St. Vincent De Paul of Baltimore*, 88-89.

14   Sandler, *The Neighborhood*, 27. It is interesting to note that some Italians continued to worship at St. Vincent's (see Spalding and Kuranda, *St. Vincent De Paul of Baltimore*, 111).

15 See website for Enoch Pratt Free Library, http://www.mdch.org/fire/.

16 Quoted in Sandler, *The Neighborhood*, 29.

17 *Church of St. Leo the Great, Celebrating 120 Years of History and Heritage* (Baltimore: Church of St. Leo the Great Press, 2001), 27-28.

18 Quoted in Sandler, *The Neighborhood*, 31.

19 Mangione and Morreale, *La Storia*, 90.

20 Ibid., 124. See also Thomas Kessner, *The Golden Door: Italian and Jewish Immigrant Mobility in New York City, 1880-1915* (New York: Oxford University Press, 1977), 5.

21 Mangione and Morreale, *La Storia*, 89.

22 Ida Esposito interview, June 28, 1979, East Baltimore Oral History Collection, Langsdale Library Special Collections, University of Baltimore.

23 Esposito interview. For discussion of the Italian-American practice of urban gardening, see Hasia R. Diner, *Hungering for America: Italian, Irish, and Jewish Foodways in the Age of Migration* (Cambridge: Harvard University Press, 2001), 62. For discussion of street socializing, see Sandler, *The Neighborhood*, 10.

24 Chiapparelli quoted in Sandler, *The Neighborhood*, 11; Frank Verde interview, February 16, 2007, conducted by author at the Sons of Italy Lodge, Baltimore.

25 Aaron Smelkinson interview, July 9, 2004, OH 620, Jewish Museum of Maryland (hereafter JMM). See also Milton Schwartz interview, November 9, 2005, OH 676, JMM; Martin Lev interview, November 4, 1980, OH 301, JMM.

26 U.S. Census Bureau, Baltimore City Manuscript Census, 1900.

27 Earl Pruce, *Synagogues, Temples, and Congregations of Maryland: 1830-1990* (Baltimore: Jewish Historical Society of Maryland, 1993).

28 *Baltimore City Directories* (Baltimore: R.L. Polk & Company, 1937, 1942); Esposito interview; Joseph Sergi interview, August 21, 1979, East Baltimore Oral History Collection, Langsdale Library Special Collections, University of Baltimore.

29 Louis Schwartz interview, July 21, 1979, Baltimore Neighborhood Heritage Project, Langsdale Library Special Collections, University of Baltimore.

30 Joseph Sergi interview, August 21, 1979, East Baltimore Oral History Collection, Langsdale Library Special Collections, University of Baltimore. Ferretti quoted in videotape of the Bath House Reunion at the Sons of Italy Lodge, recorded by Frank Verde, September 1996.

31 Mangione and Morreale, *La Storia*, 451.

32 Eric L. Goldstein, *The Price of Whiteness: Jews, Race, and American Identity* (Princeton: Princeton University Press, 2006), 41-42.

33 Marilyn Thornton Williams, "Philanthropy in the Progressive Era: The Public Baths of Baltimore," *Maryland Historical Magazine* (Spring 1977): 118.

34 Ibid.,122.

35 Ibid.,124-125.

36 Ibid.,118.

37 "Our Man Finds Best Nickel Buy in Town—City-Sponsored Bath," *Baltimore Evening Sun*, June 7, 1951.

38 Walters Bath No. 2 opened in 1901 in southwest Baltimore. These first two bath houses were restricted to whites. Walters Bath No. 3, for blacks, opened in West Baltimore in 1905. Eventually other bath houses opened as well. Solomon Liss, "Public Baths and the 1-Minute Warning," *Sun Magazine*, October 15, 1976; Williams, "Philanthropy in the Progressive Era," 127.

39 Carl Schoettler, "A Shower of Memories," *Baltimore Sun*, September 30, 1996; Williams, "Philanthropy in the Progressive Era," 127, 130.

40 "Only Two Delis and the Smell of Corned Beef Mark the Spot," unidentified newspaper, October 23, 1987, Vertical Files, Maryland Room, Enoch Pratt Free Library (hereafter EPFL); Schoettler, "A Shower of Memories."

41 Bath House Reunion videotape.

42 Ibid.

43 On this topic see for example Kessner, *The Golden Door*.

44 Shirley Yacobani, April 11, 2007, telephone interview by Juliana Ochs.

45 Lucy Vecera interview, November 11, 2006, OH 694, JMM; Louis Schwartz interview.

46 "Italian Villa Scores Hit with the Patrons," *Baltimore Jewish Times*, December 4, 1936, 19.

47 Alex Ball, et al., "That's Amore!" *Baltimore Magazine* (July 2005). Section head quote is from page 92.

48 Gilbert Sandler, "Little Italy: It's St. Leo's, Ex-Mayor Tommy, Pasta, Wine and Love of Life," *Baltimore Sun*, December 14, 1969.

49 Ibid.

50 See Mangione and Morreale, *La Storia*, 318-322.

51 Sandler, *The Neighborhood*, 41.

52 See Mangione and Morreale, *La Storia*, 321-322.

53 See article in this catalog by Deborah R. Weiner, "Public Notions, Private Lives: The Meanings of Place in an Inner City Neighborhood."

54 Ibid.

55 Unidentified article from the *Baltimore Sun*, by David Friedman, April 4, 1968.

56 Elizabeth Fee, Linda Shopes, and Linda Zeidman, eds., *The Baltimore Book: New Views on Local History* (Philadelphia: Temple University Press, 1993).

57 "Little Italy: A Sense of Belonging," unidentified newspaper, May 31, 1974, Vertical Files, Maryland Department, EPFL.

58 Article from unidentified print source, September 4, 1975, "Italians in Baltimore" Folder, Vertical Files, Maryland Department, EPFL.

59 Philip V. Cannistraro, *The Italians of New York: Five Centuries of Struggle and Achievement* (New York: The New York Historical Society and the John D. Calandra Italian American Institute, 1999), 123, 127; E. Anthony Rotundo, "Wonderbread and Stugots: Italian American Manhood and the Sopranos," in *A Sitdown with the Sopranos*, ed. Regina Barreca (New York: Palgrave MacMillan, 2002), 47-48.

60 Quoted in Sandler, *The Neighborhood*, 20-21.

61 Alex Ball, "Father Figure," *Baltimore Magazine* (July 2005): 118.

62 Paul Mugavero Baker, *La Famiglia Americana* (Baltimore, 2002), 100.

63 Ball, "Father Figure," 118.

64 Father Michael Salerno interview, February 14, 2005, conducted by author at St. Leo's Church.

65 Ball, "Father Figure," 118.

66 For the article that resulted, see "A Cinemaic Paradiso in a Bit of Old Baltimore," *New York Times*, August 11, 1999.

67 Donna R. Gabaccia, "Inventing Little Italy," www.historycooperative.org/journals/jga/6.1/gabaccia.html (reproduction of article from *Journal of the Gilded Age and Progressive Era* 6, No. 1).

68 Mangione and Morreale, *La Storia*, 461-462.

PASTRAMI 145
SHRIMP 175
HOT DOG 75
RICE PUDOING ½ PT

CORNED BEEF 549
HOT DOGS 249
PASTRAMI 395
SALAMI OR BOLOGNA 299

Public Notions, Private Lives

The Meanings of Place in an Inner City Neighborhood

European Kosher HOT DOGS ONLY 249¢ LB

Reynolds

COME IN AND BE SEATED enjoy your LUNCH IN COOL COMFORT

Public Notions, Private Lives: The Meanings of Place in an Inner City Neighborhood

BY DEBORAH R. WEINER

*F*une 1950, the exact midpoint of the twentieth century, proved to be a pivotal moment for the neighborhood located just east of downtown Baltimore, across the Jones Falls. The City Council voted by an overwhelming twenty to one margin to demolish a large portion of the housing stock in this area of "slum and blight." To replace it, the Council approved the construction of two new public housing developments featuring the latest innovation in housing for the poor: high rise buildings. In an era of legal segregation, one development was designated for whites, the other for blacks.[1]

Fast-forward to the dawn of the twenty-first century. In February 2001, with public approval seemingly as near-unanimous as that City Council vote, city officials presided over the demolition of Flag House Courts, the second of the two housing complexes authorized that June day in 1950. (The first, Lafayette Courts, had been demolished in 1995.) To replace Flag House Courts, plans called for the construction of rowhouses designed to look similar to the buildings that had been torn down a half-century earlier.[2]

The irony is obvious, but the various meanings to be gleaned from this history are less so. From today's perspective it seems clear that the wholesale "slum clearance" of old rowhouses was bad policy and that isolating the poor in high-rise buildings was destined to fail. But a close look at what happened in the neighborhood before, during, and after those two watershed events in 1950 and 2001 yields additional insights about trends and policies that have shaped urban America. And delving into how the neighborhood was perceived, experienced, and interpreted through this era—by residents, by outsiders, by policymakers and the media—helps reveal the ways that people construct community, the different meanings that can accumulate around a particular place, and the connections between past and present.

A PLACE WITH NO NAME

To have a coherent discussion about a place, it is usually customary to establish its identity and, if necessary, to define its boundaries. Immediately, then, discourse about the neighborhood "located just east of downtown Baltimore" runs into a problem. This area bounded by the Jones Falls on the west, the very-well-identified Little Italy below Pratt Street on the south, and the formerly-thriving commercial district known as Old Town on the north has had no fixed name or identity through most of its long and eventful history.

Once a fashionable residential district that some historians have described as Baltimore's first real neighborhood, by the mid-nineteenth century the area had become home to working class immigrants and African Americans. It started the twentieth century as the city's Jewish immigrant ghetto, except for its northern edge, which was predominantly black. Yet the area was not rigidly segregated, as Jews, blacks, Italians, and others could be found throughout. By the mid twentieth century many knew the place as "Jewtown"—undoubtedly

Deborah R. Weiner, Ph.D., is Research Historian and Family History Coordinator at the Jewish Museum of Maryland.

OVERLEAF: *Attmann's Delicatessen, 1979.*

Photo by Elinor B. Cahn, JMM 1985.31.5

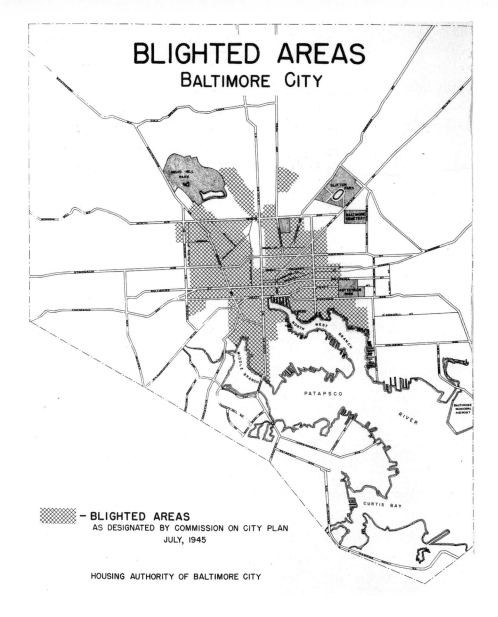

BLIGHTED AREAS
BALTIMORE CITY

▨ — **BLIGHTED AREAS**
AS DESIGNATED BY COMMISSION ON CITY PLAN
JULY, 1945

HOUSING AUTHORITY OF BALTIMORE CITY

because of the Jewish flavor of its thriving Lombard Street commercial corridor, since most Jewish residents had actually moved away by then. Shortly thereafter, the area's southern, formerly Jewish section became known by its "project" name, Flag House Courts (which in turn had been named for the landmark home that sat beside it), while the northern portion became identified with Lafayette Courts.[3]

Recognizing that the neighborhood had neither a geographic definition nor explicit boundaries, community activists in 1974 created both. As neighborhood leader Father Richard Lawrence put it, they "filled the hole in the donut" between Little Italy, downtown, Old Town, and the neighborhood of Washington Hill east of Central Avenue. They resurrected the name "Jonestown" after the area's first and long-forgotten eighteenth-century incarnation, formed the Jonestown Planning Council, and convinced city planners to designate "Jonestown" an official city neighborhood.[4]

Nearly the entire central city was labeled "blighted" by city officials in 1945.

From a Housing Authority of Baltimore City publication, courtesy of the Enoch Pratt Free Library, Central Library/State Resource Center

South High Street between Baltimore and Lombard, 1934. The neighborhood was already considered by city officials to be "slum and blighted."

Courtesy of Jacques Kelly

If Jonestown historically lacked a coherent identity, its chief characteristic was fixed in the public mind for most of the twentieth century: it was a slum. First as an immigrant ghetto, then as an ethnically and racially mixed area of dilapidated housing, then as home to two of the city's largest public housing projects, Jonestown was a place where poor people lived. This simple fact did not prevent the neighborhood from eliciting complicated responses from outsiders. It served as a blighted place to fix, a nostalgic place to relive old memories, a dangerous place to avoid, an exotic place to eat deli. Its residents too reacted to the neighborhood in diverse ways. For some it was a place to escape from. For others it was a place to act out against. For many it was a place to raise families and build community, sometimes in surprising ways.

A Neighborhood of "Slum and Blight": 1930 to 1955

Around the time of the 1950 City Council vote, Jonestown's identity was particularly unstable. Its role as a Jewish immigrant enclave had begun to fade in the 1920s, as the U.S. shut the door on immigration from Eastern Europe and those who had arrived in past decades (or their grown children) started to move away. At first, many did not go far, simply extending the Jewish presence for about a mile to the east. So although Jews no longer constituted the majority of residents in the old core neighborhood by 1930, the communal institutions located there continued to serve a large constituency. The next two decades saw a more decisive change, as Jewish outposts in the city's northwest neighborhoods and nascent suburban areas beckoned. "In the late thirties, the neighborhood changed completely," recalls Norma Livov Wolod, whose

This view of South Spring Street at mid century shows the condition of some of the neighborhood's housing.

Photo by A. Aubrey Bodine, copyright Jennifer B. Bodine, courtesy of www.aaubreybodine.com

family resisted the trend. "It was an exodus, it really was. All of my friends and their families moved away, either to the North Avenue area or the Park Heights Avenue area. . . . People just were bettering themselves. That's what it was, mainly." By 1947, only 9 percent of Baltimore's Jews still lived in East Baltimore, the former heart of the city's Jewish community.[5]

East Baltimore's Jews were participating in the early stages of a national phenomenon: the flight to suburbia, which would have a pronounced impact on inner city neighborhoods such as Jonestown. As the real estate industry poured resources into outlying areas, urban cores languished. Government actions propelled this trend, starting with the New Deal creation of the Federal Housing Administration in 1934 (whose home loan policies enabled widespread homeownership across America, while explicitly favoring white suburbs) and escalating in the post-World War II era with, for example, the infusion of federal dollars for highways.[6]

But inner cities were not totally forgotten. Ever since the turn of the twentieth century, housing reformers had fought to improve living conditions for the urban poor. Their vivid journalistic exposés had convinced the public of the evils of slum housing, yet they had little to show for their efforts. Finally, in the midst of the Depression and after President Roosevelt declared one-third of the nation "ill-housed, ill-clad, and ill-nourished," they managed to carve out a niche in the New Deal. The 1937 National Housing Act created a public housing program that offered federal funds to local governments to develop and operate low-rent housing.[7]

To surmount ferocious opposition from a powerful real estate industry intent on keeping the nation's housing market to itself (not to mention

"CLOSING NIGHT AT THE JEA"

You are cordially invited to attend the
CLOSING CEREMONIES
of the
JEWISH EDUCATIONAL ALLIANCE BUILDING
TUESDAY, NOVEMBER 11, 1952 AT 8:15 P. M.
to be held at the
JEA BUILDING - 1216 E. BALTIMORE STREET
JOSEPH SHERBOW, *Master of Ceremonies*
HERBERT L. MOSES, *Chairman of Arrangements Committee*
To commemorate the end of a past era and the beginning
of a new one.

The closing of the much-beloved Jewish Educational Alliance on East Baltimore Street confirmed that the era of "Jewish East Baltimore" had come to a close.

Gift of Joe Snyder, JMM 1995.132.1

118

conservatives who considered government-owned housing "socialistic"), the Act incorporated a series of compromises that would shape the future of public housing. For many years, local and national advocates had used the powerful idea of "slum clearance" to build support for housing legislation. The idea of eradicating the "blight" of the inner cities appealed to the public, while local officials and business leaders could see the potential economic benefits of redeveloping deteriorated areas. As a result, the Act required the elimination of one unit of slum housing for every new unit of public housing built. Equally important, the Act stipulated that public housing be limited to serving only the very poor, so as not to compete with the private sector.[8]

In their attempt to sway the public to the cause of housing reform, civic leaders used language that at times bordered on hysteria to describe the dangers of dilapidated housing. "The fact must be driven home that almost all blighted or slum areas are bankrupt areas of which cities must rid themselves as quickly as possible," a Baltimore commission blared in 1934. "Such areas are like festering sores, spreading their contagion to all contiguous territory. . . . They must be tolerated no longer than necessary."[9] Perhaps such language contributed to the alacrity with which elected officials (such as those 1950 City Council members), city agencies, journalists, civic leaders, and housing reformers endorsed turning longstanding neighborhoods into vast demolition zones. Whether or not they convinced the public, they certainly appear to have convinced themselves. As for officials of the new Housing Authority of Baltimore City (HABC), their mandate was to build—and the fierce resistance they confronted from real estate interests when they tried to acquire vacant land in outlying areas no doubt added to their zeal to obtain and transform more readily available slum properties.[10]

Such resistance was lacking in neighborhoods such as Jonestown. After losing a bruising battle to acquire an abandoned cemetery site on the city's edge, housing authority director Oliver Winston marveled at the ease with which the authority acquired the future sites of Flag House and Lafayette Courts. "Opposition was negligible considering the fact that displacement of about 1,000 families on the two sites is involved," he noted. "Opposition was confined, for the most part, to a few property owners who had natural anxieties as to how they will be compensated."[11]

Paul Wartzman's recollection reveals the ambivalence of at least some of those property owners. For years, his family had operated a bakery on Lombard Street and lived above their shop. "Our street, beginning at Exeter and Lombard Street, down to past High Street, became public housing. So they started to condemn properties. And I'll never forget, for this huge townhouse, housing a bakery, we got $19,000. But that's what my father retired on, because he never went back into the business. . . . Most of the Jews were out by that time, and the merchants who had stores did not live there anymore. We did, up until the time they condemned it."[12]

The merchants may no longer have lived on Lombard Street, but their

businesses continued to thrive even as the area around them changed. As always, they served the surrounding residents, but they also catered to a more upscale clientele of second-generation Jews who came back to the neighborhood to shop for traditional foods and literally get a taste of the old country. A 1946 newspaper article captured the changing dynamics of Lombard Street. "You used to see the old bewigged, beshawled ladies sitting on packing boxes on the curb picking chickens, and the old, skull-capped men either reading their prayer books or walking, with their eyes on the ground. It looks as though the younger generation has taken over this strip of the 'Old World.' Smart-looking matrons on stilt-like heels direct the clerks in the arrangement of wares. Prosperous-looking businessmen shout instructions. A far cry from the Lombard Street of ten years ago. Still, nonetheless fascinating."[13]

If few Jews remained in the neighborhood, who did live in Jonestown from the late 1930s to the early 1950s? As in previous decades, the northern portion (from Fayette Street to Orleans Street) tended to be African American, while the southern portion (between Fayette and Pratt) tended to be white (see map on inside front and back covers). City directories suggest that the white population was ethnically mixed, with Italians as the largest

Herman Wartzman and his niece, Esther Levin, outside Wartzman's bakery at Lombard and Front Streets in 1945. Eight years later, the building was demolished by the city to make way for public housing.

Courtesy of Paul and Rick Wartzman

These row houses on the 1000 block of Forrest Street, 1939, were typical of the housing available to African Americans in East Baltimore.

Courtesy of the Enoch Pratt Free Library, Central Library/State Resource Center

group. Between 1940 and 1950, the number of white households declined while the number of black households grew, so that the percentage of African Americans increased in the southern section from 10 to 30 percent.[14]

The transformation of the Carroll Mansion on Lombard Street reflects how the neighborhood changed and sheds light on the racial dynamics of the time. By 1900, this former home of one of Baltimore's most prominent families had become an overcrowded tenement complete with sweatshops and inhabited mostly by Jews. The City acquired the property and eventually opened a recreation center for the children of Little Italy and Jonestown. In 1940, the center served some 1,500 children, mostly Italians but also "Bohemian-Americans, Russian-Americans, and some Jewish youngsters," reported the *Baltimore Sun.* African Americans were excluded from the Carroll Mansion and their recreational opportunities were limited. They could attend the McKim Center, another landmark neighborhood institution, during certain days of the week, with whites attending on other days. In 1945, the East Side Community Committee, a Negro community organization whose territory included the northern part of Jonestown, noted that McKim's play area was very small and that East Baltimore's black district "actually does not contain a single recreational area worth the name."[15]

Despite the *Sun*'s depiction of the neighborhood as "crowded," the vacancy rate in the southern portion of Jonestown had risen to 11 percent at the time of the 1940 census. As war workers flooded into the city, this trend reversed and the worn housing stock saw an influx of residents. Most were tenants: only 20 percent of householders in the southern section owned their homes in 1940, and that percentage dropped to 16 percent by 1950.[16]

Census figures reveal a neighborhood housing stock that was old and not modernized, but not necessarily decrepit. Virtually all the structures dated from before 1900, and fully 60 percent of homes between Fayette and Pratt streets did not have private baths in 1940. Yet only 15 percent needed repair, according to the census. In 1950, 32 percent of the homes either had no running water or were dilapidated. To turn that statistic around, 68 percent of the homes had running water (though many fewer had private baths) and were not considered dilapidated.[17]

A 1937 newspaper article observed that the area "was regarded as blighted." But the threadbare housing at least offered affordability to residents suffering through the Depression. "You can rent a four-bedroom house on one of the side streets for as little as $3 a week," the article noted. "But it isn't much of a house. It has cold running water, no heat and an outside toilet. The kitchen range is a coal stove. If you want a gas stove you must buy it yourself." A gloomy local resident showed the reporter around. "'Those houses over there,' said Mr. Dickman, nodding toward the unlovely rears of St. Matthew Street, 'aren't worth anything. It would be nice if the city would buy them and put one of those housing projects over there. It would attract a higher class of people.'"[18]

Looking back, Lucille Gorham acknowledged the poor conditions but came to the opposite conclusion. She grew up on the northeast edge of the neighborhood in the 1930s and 1940s. "Housing was bad because families lived, you know, huddled up together," she recalls. "We burned wood and coal for heat. We had one big pot-bellied stove in the dining room that heated up the whole house. Your third floor was usually cold. . . . That was what was available to black people at that time." Nonetheless, "we didn't think it was a bad way of living, because all of the families lived that way. We were all poor together and we were just having fun together. I resented the city coming in and saying that this was a slum area and it's got to be torn down. I always thought you could build houses new and still keep a neighborhood intact. They just broke up neighborhoods, people moved away. You didn't know where they moved to."[19]

The notion that "slum" neighborhoods might function as real communities with social networks that helped people cope with poverty did not occur to Baltimore housing and planning officials. Convinced that bad housing equaled social pathology, their solution was to tear down the old and build up the new. In carrying out their plans, not only did they disrupt networks of family and neighbors who drew support from each other, they also contributed to the very dilemma they were attempting to solve: the lack of affordable housing for the poor. Because the time lag between tearing down and building up lasted many years, displaced residents were thrown onto an overburdened housing market, and relocation assistance provided by the HABC did little to ameliorate their plight. Community and civil rights groups supported public housing as part of the solution to Baltimore's undeniably severe housing problems. They also agreed with the housing authority on the need for recreational and social services, especially for a black population that had long suffered from discrimination in both the public and private sectors. Yet, they found themselves at odds with the authority over its heavy-handed approach, and objected to "slum clearance" policies that disproportionately dislocated African Americans.[20]

Even in the midst of World War II, with Baltimore suffering "the largest and most acute housing shortage in its history," the housing authority persisted in acquiring dilapidated housing and evicting the tenants with an eye toward future development. When critics urged the authority to allow some of its stockpiled homes to be renovated and put back into productive use, officials refused, contending that "rehabilitated houses would become slums all over again in no more than ten years." Indeed, this enthusiasm for tearing things down led the Baltimore Planning Commission to declare virtually the entire central city to be "slum and blighted" in 1945, including such modern-day fashionable rowhouse neighborhoods as Bolton Hill, Federal Hill, Fells Point, Butchers Hill, and Canton (see map on page 115).[21]

Fortunately, the housing authority did not have the resources to tear down

Houses being demolished to make way for the construction of Flag House Courts, 1953.

Courtesy of the Baltimore Sun Company, Inc., All Rights Reserved

122

all these neighborhoods. But when federal funds again became available after the war, it embarked on an ambitious new building program, choosing to start with the future sites of Lafayette and Flag House Courts, located almost adjacent to each other in "one of the worst slum areas of the city." These sites also happened to be relatively close to two projects built during the first round of public housing development in the late 1930s: the low-rise Clarence Perkins Homes (for whites) and Frederick Douglass Homes (for blacks). The HABC planned to duplicate many of the features it had instituted in these developments, including largely successful programs that offered health care, child care, recreation, and other activities.[22]

But in two important ways, the new projects would be different. First, rising land costs and bold new ideas in architecture combined to usher in the era of the high rise. As HABC Development Director Philip Darling explained in 1952, "Slum sites have become so expensive that more dwelling units per acre are needed to absorb site acquisition costs." Rather than increase the density on the ground, HABC planners decided to build up. Elevator buildings would allow "more open space between buildings and increase the area which can be devoted to landscaping and recreational uses." In turning to the high rise, Darling and public housing officials across the nation followed influential Modernist architects who recommended high rise public housing to prevent "crowded-on-the-ground city districts" and to provide "more light, air, and tranquility, and better view." Some longtime public housing advocates objected that elevator buildings were unsuitable for families and that too many people were being packed into too small a space, but the expediency of the high rise, accompanied by the gloss of architectural innovation, carried the day.[23]

Second, the Supreme Court decisions outlawing segregation in 1954 caused the HABC to desegregate its public housing by following a "policy of preference" that allowed applicants to apply to the project of their choice without racial restriction. Lafayette Courts, which replaced rowhouses occupied largely by blacks, had few white applicants and remained virtually all-black from its inception. But of the 378 households displaced by Flag House Courts, some 65 percent were white, many of Italian background. Originally designated for whites, the project had received the support of local City Councilman Joseph Bertorelli. It would open with a racially integrated population.[24]

City Councilman Joseph Bertorelli, Mayor Tommy D'Alesandro, Jr., and an unidentified official pose at the groundbreaking ceremony for Flag House Courts in February 1954.

123

AN INNER CITY COMMUNITY, 1955-1968

In May 1953, after the housing authority spent almost three years acquiring land and removing residents, city officials gathered at the site of the future Flag House Courts to announce the start of the demolition phase. Mayor Thomas D'Alesandro, Jr., a product of Little Italy and firm supporter of public housing, called it "a great day for the city of Baltimore" as he pulled down a "carefully weakened" brick wall. A housing authority official noted that almost all the residents had been relocated from the area, remarking, "Look around you and you'll see that they needed relocation." Four days later, a reporter toured the uninhabited expanse of land, describing it as "a ghost town, in the center of a huge city." Soon would arise three massive twelve-story buildings and fifteen three-story buildings totaling 487 apartments.[25]

When both Flag House Courts and the much larger Lafayette Courts (816 apartments) opened in 1955, the area was suddenly repopulated. The HABC's attitude toward the former "slum site" took an abrupt turn, as it now touted the "many advantages" of the neighborhood: proximity to schools, churches, Johns Hopkins Hospital, and several shopping areas, especially the one right in the midst of Flag House Courts. "Residents . . . have their pick of all kinds of food in the Lombard Street stores," an HABC brochure enthused.[26]

Most of all, though, the housing authority extolled the modern features of its new developments. "Flag House Courts, a garden spot in the heart of East Baltimore, is the second project of the HABC to soar high into the air," the brochure proclaimed. It noted the project's fully equipped kitchens, modern bathrooms, and common areas that included basement laundry rooms and high rise play areas: "tot lots in the sky" that ensured that "mothers need not interrupt a busy day to take young children downstairs to the outdoor playgrounds." The housing authority particularly delighted in the vistas that rivaled those of pricey penthouse apartments. There was "no better view of activities in the harbor anywhere," a press release noted.[27]

One reporter who toured Lafayette Courts was not completely impressed. "Outwardly, the brick facing looks indistinguishable from the exterior of luxury apartment houses," he observed. "On the inside, the differences are striking." Limited in its budget, the HABC had made some compromises. Floors were concrete, rather than wood or tile. Closets were recessed alcoves with no doors. Outdoor corridors and play areas, although they provided space for people to gather and children to play, had to be screened with heavy-duty mesh to prevent accidents, and the long fenced-in corridors "give something of the effect of a well-kept prison."[28]

But to people accustomed to overcrowded and sagging rowhouses that lacked indoor bathrooms, the new public housing complexes that ringed downtown Baltimore promised a major improvement in living standards. The HABC received thousands of applications every year (in 1953, it had more than 11,000 applications on file), and the fraction who managed to obtain apartments considered themselves fortunate. Applicants went through a selective screening process that added to the residents' sense of achieving a significant step up.[29]

John Maggio, his wife, and four children became the first family to move into Flag House Courts in November 1955. Maggio told a reporter that the new apartment "was like the answer to a dream for his large family. Two of his children had been forced to sleep in the living room of the dilapidated house they left." The Maggio family was part of Flag's initial white majority; in 1960, 60 percent of the households were white, making it one of the HABC's

John Maggio posing for the cameras as he enters his new home at Flag House Courts in November 1955. The Maggio family was the first to move into the development.

Courtesy of the Baltimore Sun Company, Inc., All Rights Reserved

124

more racially-balanced projects.[30] While the HABC had confronted white resistance and racial tension when it integrated its older, white-only projects, former residents recall that race relations at Flag were basically good. "When I moved there, it was wonderful," says Esther Dortch, an African American who came in 1961. "It was black and white folks, you know, all lived down there together." Charles Dingle grew up in Flag and played with white children, including a boy named Randy who was like a brother to him and whose mother invited him to the family's large birthday parties with a friendly, "Come in, child."[31]

But black-white interaction was not always harmonious, and in any case would not last long. As Dingle recalls, childhood play could take an ugly turn. When spats broke out, "then somebody gotta call you nigger, and there it'd go." Each year more whites moved out than blacks, and replacements tended to be black. Bigotry on the part of white tenants may have played a role, but more important, job and housing discrimination made the path out of public housing less accessible for blacks than for whites. As the HABC noted, "White families have a greater opportunity to improve their wage-earning prospects quickly and have a much greater choice of housing accommodations." By 1970, 97 percent of Flag households were black.[32]

For young African American families of the postwar baby boom era, public housing offered a way to start life afresh in a new environment, in somewhat the same way that young white couples were leaving older city neighborhoods for the suburbs. Whereas white families received aid to do so from FHA and GI Bill home loans, exclusionary policies prevented many blacks—even veterans—from accessing these government benefits.[33] After Ann Faulkner Evans moved into the tenth floor of a Flag House Courts high rise in 1962, she quickly got to know her neighbors. "It was young people like myself that had babies. Basically, they was married. It was just a nice, clean place." At the time she moved in, she had one child with another on the way. Her husband, a Navy veteran who worked as a stock clerk, made the decision to apply. "He figured it was a little hard on him 'cause his pay wasn't [sufficient] to keep up with the [decent] apartments" available on the private market. "And then we needed more space." Evans's family was typical of Flag households during that time: in 1961, half of the households consisted of two-parent families with children, 28 percent were single-parent households, and the remainder were elderly or adults with no children.[34]

In the early years, Flag residents enjoyed their new homes, had few complaints about the upkeep, and appreciated the amenities. "It was beautiful," recalls Evans. "The maintenance was so good. Only thing was, I was scared of the elevators because I wasn't used to being up high like that." Esther Dortch lived in a Flag low rise. "I had a beautiful yard, beautiful

View of Flag House Courts in 1956, showing playgrounds, basketball courts, and three of the project's twelve low rise buildings.

126

flowers. I planted some vegetables even . . . bell peppers, cucumbers, tomatoes, greens. I had a white picket fence, my son built that." Evelyn Scipio arrived in 1963. "It was a nice little community," she later told a reporter. "We had the [mobile] swimming pool that would come around for the kids. There were swings, camps, the Boy Scouts. The managers at the time, they were concerned about people, about the place. You couldn't even leave the clothes outdoors to dry. Somebody in management would take them down. They said it was unsightly." They also were diligent about upkeep. Flag was "very, very clean," asserts Dorothy Scott. "We had maintenance men that would mop the stairwells everyday from the top floor all the way down."[35]

Children turned the dark, fenced-in high-rise tot lots into noisy play areas. "You'd be surprised," says Scott. "There was a fence, but it was a big open area. And that's where the children rode their bicycles. . . . They played baseball and the front of the tot lot would be home, [then there was] first base, second base and then you had the outfield, which was the elevator lobby." But parents also took their children down to the playground, because "we just didn't want our children to be pent up in the building."[36]

People who lived in Flag during the 1960s and 1970s recall a close-knit community of neighbors who helped each other out. "When we first moved there it was like having a big family on your floor," says Sheila Rosemond, who came to Flag as a child in 1970. "Everybody stuck together. We borrowed stuff from each other. . . . Everybody listened to everybody else's mom because they might discipline you." Residents also worked together in formal organizations, sometimes in cooperation with management and sometimes in opposition. Dorothy Scott, who started her community activism with youth programs and became longtime president of the tenants' council, recalls a variety of activities available to her as a young mother in the 1970s. "We had a community action agency downstairs in the building. There was a library where you could take your kids, and a food coop. And we as residents, I had one child, my neighbor might have two, we would buy in bulk," and gather together to distribute their foodstuffs. "It was a good community. Flag House was a pleasant place to live at one point in time."[37]

But what about the surrounding community? The designers of modern public housing, intent on creating something new and bold, apparently gave little thought to how their hulking buildings would relate to the environment—if anything, most public housing complexes appear to be self-contained, deliberately turning their backs on the street life around them. When Flag House Courts was built, the street grid was broken up so that many streets did not go into or through the development: on a map one can see how they stopped at one end and resumed at the other end, leaving a blank space in the middle. The only street that sliced through the projects was Lombard Street. Planners probably would have truncated Lombard as well, but they could not. It served as a "through" street necessary for traffic patterns—and in addition, the blocks that passed through Flag made up the heart of the

Flag House Courts high rise, circa 1976.
Courtesy of the Baltimore City Commission for Historical and Architectural Preservation

127

Lombard Street commercial district.

And Lombard Street in the 1950s and 1960s continued to thrive. Jewish and Italian merchants, sons and daughters of the immigrants who first set up shop there, carried on the tradition "with the same spirit, love of life and desire to please," as one mid-1960s newspaper article put it. Stone's Bakery, Attman's deli, the groceries of Pastore and Garafalo, Faiman's clothing store, Ginsburg's produce store, Tony's fruit market, Yankelove's "kill-while-you-wait" poultry store, Smelkinson's dairy, and many other shops crowded one another, their wares spilling out into streets that on weekends were filled with shoppers. The street's mantra, as articulated by Harry Attman, remained the same as always: "Selling is like shaving. If you don't do it every day you're a bum!"[38]

Despite the physical barriers imposed by the design of Flag House Courts, residents integrated Lombard Street into their lives and it became a major part of their community. As for the merchants, they apparently appreciated regaining a neighborhood clientele after several years of operating within a "ghost town." Although most depended for their livelihoods on shoppers traveling to their stores from across Baltimore, they responded readily to this new local market for their wares. They were joined by new merchants, often Korean Americans, who catered primarily to the neighborhood. Flag residents patronized all these stores. As Dorothy Scott puts it, Lombard Street was "people friendly. . . . The stores were always good to the community."[39]

In any case, merchants were becoming used to an increasingly African American clientele. The heart of black East Baltimore was located just to the north and east, and its residents began to patronize its stores regularly in the postwar era. "I used to go down to Jewtown every Sunday morning," says Julia Matthews, who lived near Orleans Street. "We liked going down there. We liked to get those fresh chickens, pickles . . ." Local residents appreciated having a thriving shopping district with a wide variety of stores within walking distance—and the opportunity to buy live chickens that were slaughtered on site was especially valued by black customers, many of whom had migrated to Baltimore from the rural South. Esther Dortch's memories of Flag are tied up with her memories of Lombard Street, in which chickens figure prominently. "I loved Flag House, tell you the truth and I loved it that you come down here to these stores, get fresh chickens killed and good fresh eggs. . . . Fresh chicken always tastes better than store chicken." As Julia Matthews explains, "It was just like those country chickens, I guess."[40]

Matthews recalls that relations between African American shoppers and merchants were "good, good, good. You didn't hear no cussing words. They would joke with you, the Jewish and some of the African American people that would work with the Jewish people, they knew some of the [Yiddish] words and they would joke and they would laugh." Lombard Street businesses employed African Americans in a variety of jobs. Thelma Lovelace worked at Tulkoff's horseradish plant, packing jars into cardboard boxes. She

A worker outside of Yankelove's poultry store at 1012 East Lombard Street, 1963.

Photo by John McGrain, gift of John McGrain, JMM 1995.187.15

128

appreciated the money, though conditions were less than ideal. Her brother slaughtered chickens for one of the chicken dealers. They called him Joe, though that was not in fact his name. But "he loved them and they loved him." Some merchants hired local children to do odd jobs. Recalls Charles Dingle, "I worked in almost all the stores down there" as a young boy. "I wanted to be like my father. You know, he was a working man. So I went around the corner every morning. 'Hey, mister, you need some help today?' Ginsburg was the first one to hire me. Said sure, 50 cents a day. But I was happy . . . that was a hundred cookies." On the whole, neighborhood residents who worked on the street welcomed the extra income, though they felt that some of the employers exploited them.[41]

It was the buyer-seller relationship that drew residents and merchants together. The merchants, in the manner of small shopkeepers the world over, knew their customers by name. And in the manner of shopkeepers the world over who served poor people, they offered credit in times of need. "We had the store Crazy's Market," Dorothy Scott relates of one Korean American-owned store. "Awesome. Holiday time come and they knew you were trying to buy Christmas toys. They would help you out. . . . If you went and you were short, they made sure you had what you needed. Next month, you got your

Ginsburg's produce market, 1023 East Lombard Street, 1964.

Lombard Street, looking west from Central Avenue, 1968, with a Flag House Courts high rise in the background.

Courtesy of the Baltimore Sun Company, Inc., All Rights Reserved

OPPOSITE: *Lombard Street in the 1960s.*

Photo by A. Aubrey Bodine, copyright Jennifer B. Bodine, courtesy of www.aaubreybodine.com

money, you went and paid your little bill."

Some merchants became trusted figures to the local populace. Andrew Silbert, owner of a small pharmacy on the corner of Lombard and Lloyd streets, was known to his customers as "Doc." He "loved the people in the community," says Scott. After he filled prescriptions for children, he would call the parents to see how their kids were doing. Italian grocery storeowner Vince Pastore helped his customers in large ways and small. Once, when Scott's son was being chased by another boy, "He figured if he could get to Pastore's he would be safe. When he went in, he pushed the door and the glass broke. But Vince wasn't worried about the door, he was worried about him." Pastore walked the boy home to Scott. "He wasn't afraid to come in the building . . . and he brought him upstairs. And he told me what happened, and he said, 'Dorothy, he's gonna have to pay me for my door. He's gonna have to work it off.' And I said, 'Well, he'll be there after school.' And he had him sweeping and cleaning up and at the end of the day he would give him a gallon of milk and a gallon of juice. . . . So, Vince got the door fixed because he had insurance on it," but this was his way of showing concern and helping the family out. "And that was like any store on Lombard Street."[42]

If Lombard Street served as a space where merchants and shoppers could experience community across economic and racial lines, Pastore's walk over to Scott's apartment was a bold act to extend this community: an attempt to ignore the spatial divide that increasingly separated "project residents" from everyone else. There were other examples of this kind of border crossing in

the early years of Flag House Courts. Lou Catalfo, who grew up in Little Italy, used to visit an African American friend in the project, and he was not alone. "We'd play basketball on their courts and they'd play on ours," he told a reporter. "We used to go over to the high rise just to ride the elevators."[43]

Flag residents' memories of Lombard Street reveal their nostalgia for a time when the project was less isolated, more integrated into the life of the city. Whether bantering in Yiddish with their employers, watching their chickens become "fresh-killed," or marveling at the crowds who shopped on the street, they had the sense that they were included in the hustle and bustle of a diverse urban society. Says Dorothy Scott, "Every nationality was on that street, every nationality. Jews, whites, Italians, African Americans, you name it, they were there. It was just nice, because it was an open atmosphere." And like the journalists and uptowners who for years had come to Lombard Street to soak up the atmosphere, residents of Flag and adjacent black neighborhoods found the place fascinating. "You'd go down there and you'd see people from all over the city. People that had moved away from here, you would see them too," observes Julia Matthews. "You don't have no peoples walking up and down Lombard Street now, do you? . . . In Attmans' they had barrels with pickles and herring. That's a salted fish. Tomatoes, you know what pickled tomatoes are? They had them. And pickled onions, pickled cucumbers." Even though it was right around the corner, reminisces Charles Dingle, "It was like going downtown."[44]

But if Lombard Street helped connect local residents to a larger community, the neighborhood was becoming more isolated in every other way. Urban renewal continued to transform the built environment: in the early 1960s, the building of the Jones Falls Expressway and related road projects helped cut the neighborhood off from downtown. Between 1960 and 1962, the residential district between Flag House and Lafayette Courts was bulldozed to make way for an industrial park that never materialized. By destroying 234 structures, this project displaced 133 black and 74 white households and also removed commercial and industrial enterprises that had provided local jobs. The area remained vacant until the city built the new main post office in 1970.[45]

Economically and socially, poor urban neighborhoods across America were becoming more marginalized as the 1960s progressed. As the white working and middle classes decamped for the suburbs, middle-class blacks moved out of inner cities into better housing vacated by whites in more upscale neighborhoods. The poor were left with two options: a deteriorated and shrinking housing stock decimated by urban renewal—or public housing, usually filled to the brim at densities that many experts thought far too high. Meanwhile, manufacturing jobs were disappearing at a rapid rate, making poverty more difficult to escape than ever. Constricted opportunities and increased isolation led to frustration and anger in poor black communities around the nation. The growing discontent was expressed in a variety of ways: from the militant activism of the growing black power movement, to an increase in crime and violence, to the riots that broke out in many cities in the mid-1960s.[46]

RIOTS AND REBIRTH, 1968-2001

On April 6, 1968, two days after the assassination of Dr. Martin Luther King, Jr., unrest in Baltimore turned into mass disorder. The riots started with the smashing of a window on Gay Street in the Old Town commercial district just north of Jonestown and spread throughout Baltimore's ghettoes over the following three days.

Lombard Street was not spared the looting and destruction. "Tenants leaned from upper floors of the Flag House Courts public housing project as they hooted down at firemen responding to a blaze in a produce store in the 1000 block of East Lombard Street," the *Baltimore Sun* reported on April 7. "The taunts included shouts of 'We shall overcome' and 'wait until tonight.'" An article the following day described how "City police were pinned down behind their cars by two or three snipers firing down from the upper floors of the Flag House housing project. . . . Police withdrew under a hail of bottles from project residents." Minutes later, a fire broke out at Smelkinson's dairy store, which burned to the ground. One former Flag resident maintains that Smelkinson's was deliberately targeted because some residents resented what

Smelkinson's Dairy, 1017 East Lombard Street, burns during the April 1968 riots.

Courtesy of Special Collections, University of Maryland Libraries

they saw as unfair treatment. However, he observes, much of the looting was purely random, and many stores that enjoyed good relations with residents also sustained some damage.[47]

Residents such as Esther Dortch were trapped inside their apartments, fearful of rioters and law enforcement alike. "Honey, I didn't go out there to watch what was happening. I was in the house," she relates. "I had my children down on the floor," because "the National Guard was out there with guns pointed at the high rises." She worried too that her children might be hit from the stray bullets of snipers shooting down from the upper floors. On the other hand, fourteen-year-old Charles Dingle got caught up in the looting. His mother forbade him to go out, "but I snuck out there anyway. . . . And I'd go in, take a little of this, little of that. But as you get older, you realize now you wasn't doing nothing but hurting yourself. Because we needed those stores."[48]

Indeed, the upheaval spelled the beginning of the end for Lombard Street—though it did not happen right away. In fact, unlike other commercial districts hit by Baltimore's riots, most Lombard Street businesses suffered only minor damage. Aside from the totally destroyed Smelkinson's, only two liquor stores and a small food market shut down. In the month following the riots, the storeowners' main problem was a lack of customers rather than looted stores. Rumors had circulated that the entire block of 1100 East Lombard Street had burned to the ground, "leaving Baltimore's Italian and Jewish specialty delicatessens almost empty for several days," according to one newspaper account. Another noted that business "has fallen off so badly that thirteen stores placed a newspaper ad saying, 'We are open and ready to serve you.'" Merchants insisted that they would "continue the stores started by their fathers and grandfathers," with meat market owner Benny Posner asserting, "We're here to stay and we'll battle to do it."[49]

Within a month the street came back to life. A May 6 article noted, "Yesterday, Attman's delicatessen served 400 people and crowds waited in a line 200 feet long at Jack's." Though one shopkeeper told a reporter that "neighborhood residents were ashamed to return to her store, where many of their children had looted," soon the locals came back and their relationship with merchants picked up where it left off, according to former Flag residents. Baltimore's Jews continued to patronize the market of their increasingly distant immigrant past, while other Baltimoreans, white and black, continued to come in search of bargains and local color.[50]

Within a year, *Sun* reporter Ralph Reppert described the street's atmosphere almost as if nothing had ever happened. "It survives as a tiny unchanged island, noisy and odorous, of ancient, old world foods, customs, and conversation." But not quite unchanged: deep into the article he mentioned a few "gaping storefronts." He attributed their appearance not to the riots, which he downplayed, but to "old age, with no younger family generation to operate them after the old folks died."[51]

In fact, several factors came together in the post-1968 era to cause the

decline of Lombard Street. The riots, though not as physically destructive to the neighborhood as past urban renewal projects, had serious long-term consequences. "After the riots, it wasn't the same," says Charles Dingle. "The people came but it wasn't as busy." Whites felt less comfortable in the city and blacks felt more isolated than ever. Property crimes such as robbery, vandalism, and petty theft began to plague storeowners. As an Italian fruit dealer told Reppert, "Once, we make up the displays outside. Nobody steal. . . . Now we got to keep somebody at the outside stall every minute." Meanwhile, a retail revolution was underway in America, with supermarkets and malls drawing customers away from traditional shopping areas. This exacerbated the generational change noted by Reppert: the age of the small family business was drawing to a close.[52]

The final blow came, fittingly enough, with urban renewal. In 1976, Lombard Street was shut down for major road repairs as part of a citywide commercial revitalization project. For several months the street was impassable by car and treacherous for pedestrians, causing customers to stay away. "The way the city's busted up the street here, it looks like there's been a war and we've been bombed out," complained Marty Stone of Stone's Bakery. For some already-vulnerable businesses, the impact was crippling. After the street reopened, city officials touted the new, improved Lombard Street, now dubbed "Corned Beef Row." But by November of that year, twelve of twenty-eight stores were vacant, including Stone's landmark bakery. Finally, in the 1980s, boarded-up storefronts began to outnumber open businesses. By century's end, only a few stores remained.[53]

Lombard Street became a "virtual no-man's land" during major road repairs in 1976, according to one newspaper report. Several businesses closed as a result.

Courtesy of Special Collections, University of Maryland Libraries

The 1970s also proved to be difficult years for Flag House Courts and public housing nationwide. The growing crisis of the inner cities was compounded by federal housing policies. In 1969, a new law stipulated that public housing residents pay no more than 25 percent of their incomes for rent, leaving housing authorities at the mercy of the federal government to make sure they had enough funds to operate. Sure enough, in 1972 subsidies were slashed and housing authorities, unable to increase rents, became strapped for cash. Predictably, building maintenance, tenant screening, and social services suffered. Meanwhile, higher-earning residents saw their rents go up to the allowed limit—until they earned too much, in which case they were required to leave. Also, with an increasing number of residents on public assistance, the "man-in-the-house rule" imposed by welfare departments, which dictated that only single mothers with children could receive benefits, contributed to the loss of an adult male presence.[54]

The cumulative effects began to be felt at Flag. "It was family oriented when I moved in," says Dorothy Scott. "There were husbands there, there were men in the household then. But some families started moving out because the rent was going up. . . . And as people started moving out, younger mothers, unwed mothers with children were moving in." By 1977, 83 percent of residents received public assistance. That year, more than 60 percent of the population of Jonestown (consisting almost solely of Flag House and Lafayette Courts) was under the age of eighteen, compared to a city average of 34 percent. The two projects were jam-packed, with some 4,800 people living in 1,300 apartments. One housing authority report stated that of Flag's 487 units, only five were vacant.[55]

Despite population pressures and increased poverty, former Flag residents recall the 1970s fondly. A community feeling still pervaded the project and, until the latter part of the decade, Lombard Street was still quite viable. It was the 1980s, they contend, "when things started to change." Drugs were the main culprit, affecting every aspect of project life. As Scott explains, "in the late sixties and the seventies, you heard about drugs but you didn't see it."

In the 1980s, drug dealers took over the common areas, intimidating residents and management alike. "When drugs started coming in, maintenance men could not get in the buildings," says Scott. "That meant the steps wouldn't get cleaned. The incinerator got so filled up with trash that it was coming up on each floor." But worse than the trash was the violence. "It was to the point where, it was just not feasible for our children to be outside because of so much gunfire. You always heard gunshots, all the time." By 1993, a *Baltimore Sun* special report on Flag House Courts reported that "Together, [drugs and guns] have transformed Flag House into a place so wretched, where violence and death are so familiar, that it resembles a war zone." The article described a place full of fear, where law-abiding families cowered in their apartments while criminals roamed the buildings, where children and adults succumbed to the lure of drugs and crime, and where few families

136

The Jones family, Flag House Courts, summer 1994.

Photo by Japonicka Jones, BCLM photo documentary project, courtesy of The Maryland Historical Society

remained untouched by violence.[56]

In the midst of this grave situation, there were people inside and out of the project who fought to maintain their community and their families. Women such as Dorothy Scott and Ann Faulkner Evans organized after-school activities for children at the local schools, pushed the housing authority to improve security, and advocated on behalf of residents through the tenants' council. Among other things, their organizing efforts provided critical support to the community campaign that resulted in the federally-funded HOPE VI project, under which Flag House Courts was torn down and a mixed-income rowhouse development was built in its place. They then turned their attention to advocating for residents through the inevitable relocation process.[57]

Many women simply focused their efforts on raising good kids against great odds. Their success could be seen in a 1994 photography project organized by curators of the (now-defunct) Baltimore City Life Museums (BCLM), who gave neighborhood children cameras and encouraged them to record their lives. The children's vibrant photos provide an alternative narrative to the *Sun's* disturbing report on Flag House Courts. In the photos, families say grace before meals and gather outside on lawn chairs to socialize. Students do homework on computers and proud moms show off diplomas. Kids swing from poles, perform splits, and palm basketballs. They visit local merchants (who are now Asian), fix each others' hair, help with the gardening. Not all is sunny: photos of "Do Not Enter" signs and chain link fences mark the boundaries of their lives. But the pictures are full of life, not despair. These children are growing up, albeit under tough circumstances. (In later years, the young photographers would become medical clerks and hair stylists, college students and chefs.)[58]

The women of Flag House Courts weren't the only ones who fought against neighborhood decline. In the mid-1970s, Father Richard Lawrence of historic St. Vincent de Paul Church spearheaded the formation of the Jonestown Planning Council. Lawrence had a deep appreciation for the neighborhood's history and a determination to return it to its longtime role— "not to make it fancy but to have it once again become functional as a 'starter neighborhood' for the poor," as reporter Edgar Jones summarized in a profile titled "Jonestown, A Section Only a Father Could Love." The Council brought together Lombard and Baltimore Street businesses, public housing residents, social service workers, and a disparate group of preservationists working to save Jonestown's eighteenth- and nineteenth-century treasures, which had miraculously survived the past half-century of demolition and neglect.[59]

These treasures included several buildings ranged along the Front Street corridor: the Carroll Mansion, the Flag House (where the Star-Spangled Banner was sewn), the iconic Shot Tower, and the home of the third mayor of Baltimore, which had devolved into a vacant and crumbling auto repair shop. The buildings' cause was championed by groups such as the Women's Civic League and Baltimore Heritage, Inc., which began to challenge the urban renewal juggernaut and advocate for ways to bring Baltimore's unique heritage "back to life before it

Earl Cornish and Gary Outlaw at the computer, summer 1994.

Photo by Shaun Gibson, BCLM photo documentary project, courtesy of The Maryland Historical Society

137

Proprietor Seoung Rim waits on a customer at Crazy's Market on South Exeter Street, summer 1994.

Photo by Reginald Marable, BCLM photo documentary project, courtesy of The Maryland Historical Society

is lost under a blanket of contemporary steel and concrete."[60]

One group of preservationists felt a special tie to the neighborhood. In 1960, members of the city's Jewish community came together to save the historic Lloyd Street Synagogue from demolition. Dedicated to preserving East Baltimore's Jewish heritage, they did not stop there. After acquiring and renovating the decrepit synagogue in the 1960s, they built a museum beside it in the 1980s, at a time when investing in the neighborhood could only have been seen as quixotic. Meanwhile, a committed core of Orthodox Jews kept Jewish worship alive in the old neighborhood, steadfastly maintaining an active congregation at the B'nai Israel synagogue on the same block of Lloyd Street.[61]

The success of all these efforts laid the foundation for the latest transformation of the neighborhood. Oddly enough, the new-found appreciation of Jonestown's history would spread to the very forces that had abused that history so thoroughly over the past sixty years: the forces of urban renewal. In the 1990s, recognizing that high-rise public housing complexes had served to concentrate and isolate the poor, Baltimore participated in a federally-funded nationwide movement to demolish these projects. At the urging of neighborhood groups such as the Jonestown Planning Council, city officials decided to replace Flag House Courts with a mixed-income development whose design echoed the good old-fashioned Baltimore rowhouse. The newest neighborhood makeover, announced with as much fanfare as that which accompanied the creation of Flag, involved tearing down the high rises and going "back to the future," in the words of the new development's architect.[62]

EPILOGUE: THE LATEST EXPERIMENT

The demolition of Flag House Courts and the construction of "Albemarle Square" was in fact a deliberate attempt to obliterate the past half century of neighborhood history. Public housing, universally perceived to be a failure, would be wiped out and replaced by housing whose style derived from a nostalgically viewed past era, when rich and poor lived side by side in harmony (but with indoor bathrooms, and plenty of them). Of the new development's 338 housing units, 130 were reserved for former Flag House Courts residents or other public housing tenants, some fifty more were designated for people of low and moderate income, and the rest were sold at market rates and marketed to middle- and upper-middle-class professionals. Community activists accepted this diminution of low-income units as a trade-off for affordable homeownership opportunities and other features designed to assist former Flag residents.[63]

The scheme's historic intent actually leapfrogged 150 years of the neighborhood's past—as a slum. Rich and poor had not lived together in Jonestown since the mid-nineteenth century. Skepticism of the plan has come from all sides: journalists, former Flag residents, the general public. With the housing just coming on line over the past two years, it remains to be seen how this latest experiment in urban revitalization will play out.

William Jacobs doing "semis," Flag House Courts, summer 1994.

Photo by Donald Woodard, BCLM photo documentary project, courtesy of The Maryland Historical Society

In the meantime, former residents express mixed feelings about the whole thing. Though most supported the demolition of the vastly deteriorated, crime-scarred project, and though community leaders attempted to use the process to improve residents' lives, they recall past times and the opportunities that Flag House Courts had provided. "People don't realize that places like Flag House gave people a new lease on life," Dorothy Scott told a reporter who covered the events surrounding the demolition. "It's not where you live, but how you live. And we made a life here." But on demolition day, it was Scott who slammed down the ceremonial plunger that signaled the end of Flag.[64]

Charles Dingle and Ann Faulkner Evans reflect on the lost personal history that the demolition caused. "They pushed that button, you see it fall . . . man that was hurting," Dingle recalls. "Seriously, I mean, that was my home. That was old Flag House. That was my stomping grounds." Evans too watched Flag come down. "I was crying. A lot of people say, oh I'm so glad, but I wasn't." She would have preferred a renovation of the project's low and high rises, with the top floors perhaps sheared off. "The foundations were good. All they had to do was be brought up to date." Her comments echoed the words of Lucille Gorham, who lamented the destruction of the neighborhood that occurred decades earlier to make way for public housing. To both, more was lost than bricks and mortar. "See, Flag House was like a family," Evans says. "Even though we weren't perfect, you know, they was a family to me."[65]

For over a century, the lived experience of the people of Jonestown has been at odds with public perceptions of the neighborhood. As early as 1907, when Baltimore journalists and housing reformers treated the Jewish ghetto as an exotic slum filled with an "unkempt" and "unwashed" race of people who followed strange customs, residents have been viewed as the "other." Like inner city communities nationwide, Jonestown has been a place for poor people to live and for other Americans to project their views on urban life. As the neighborhood heads into the next century, that could be one thing that does not change.

NOTES

Thanks to Ed Schechter and Jerry Wittik for their invaluable assistance with research for this essay and for the *Voices of Lombard Street* exhibition.

1   *Journal of Housing* 7 (Aug 1950): 269.

2   Edward Gunts, "Plan for Community Wins National Award," *Baltimore Sun*, January 11, 2001; Michael Anft, "Flag Down: Elevated Spirits, Uncertain Prospects Accompany High Rise Implosion," *City Paper,* February 14, 2001.

3   "Jonestown Historic Designation Report," Baltimore City Commission for Historical and Architectural Preservation (hereafter CHAP), 2002; U.S. Census Bureau, Baltimore City Manuscript Census, 1900, 1920, 1930. This essay will focus on the southern section of the neighborhood, which was the heart of the former Jewish enclave that is the subject of *Voices of Lombard Street.* Flag House Courts was named for the Flag House on Pratt Street, home of Mary Pickersgill. In 1814, she and her workers sewed the flag that flew over Fort McHenry and inspired Francis Scott Key to write the Star-Spangled Banner. Today, the house is part of the Flag House & Star-Spangled Banner Museum.

4   Father Richard Lawrence, interview with author and Anita Kassof, St. Vincent de Paul Church, Baltimore, January 26, 2006; Thomas Hasler, "Jonestown Seeks To Create Image," *Baltimore Evening Sun,* September 18, 1975.

5   U.S. Census Bureau, Manuscript Census, 1920 and 1930; *Baltimore City Directories* (Baltimore: R.L. Polk & Company, 1930, 1937, 1940, 1942); Norma Livov Wolod interview, June 7, 2006, OH 687, Jewish Museum of Maryland (hereafter JMM); Associated Jewish Charities, "Study of Recreational and Informal Educational Activities, Baltimore, January 1947," JMM 1995.098. On the demographic trajectory of Baltimore's Jewish population, see for example, Gilbert Sandler, *Jewish Baltimore: A Family Album* (Baltimore: Johns Hopkins University Press, 2000).

6   The devastating impact on inner cities of FHA home loan policies from the 1930s to the 1960s (as well as the home loan policies of the enormously influential GI Bill) is detailed in Kenneth T. Jackson's classic study, *Crabgrass Frontier: The Suburbanization of the United States* (New York, Oxford University Press, 1985): 190-218.

7   Deborah R. Weiner, "From New Deal Promise to Postmodern Defeat: Two Baltimore Housing Projects," in *From Mobtown to Charm City: New Perspectives on Baltimore's Past* (Baltimore: Maryland Historical Society, 2002): 198-224.

8   Ibid.

9   Quoted in Housing Authority of Baltimore City, *Baltimore Building Low Rent Homes, First Annual Report,* 1939. All publications and reports cited in this article from Baltimore's housing, urban, and community development agencies are located in the Maryland Department, Enoch Pratt Free Library (EPFL), Baltimore, unless otherwise noted.

10   The Housing Authority of Baltimore City (HABC) was created in 1937 after passage of the National Housing Act, as the entity to receive federal funds to build and operate public housing. On opposition to its activities, see Rhonda I. Williams, *The Politics of Public Housing: Black Women's Struggles Against Urban Inequality* (New York: Oxford University Press, 2004); and Weiner, "From New Deal Promise to Postmodern Defeat."

11   On the cemetery battle, see *Journal of Housing* 7 (January 1950): 9. Quote is from *Journal of Housing* 7 (August 1950): 269.

12   Paul Wartzman interview, June 5, 2006, OH 686, JMM.

13   Carroll Delaney, "Queer Shops Found on East Lombard Street," *Baltimore News-Post,* November 22, 1946.

14   U.S. Census Bureau, U.S. Census of Housing, Maryland—Block Statistics, 1940 and 1950 (Washington: GPO); *Baltimore City Directories,* 1937, 1942.

15   "Carroll Mansion Houses Play Activities of 1,500 Kids," *Baltimore Sun*, February 25, 1940; Janel Bisacquino, "Unearthing an Urban Landscape: The Carroll-Caton Garden," unpublished report, Baltimore City Life Museums, 1995 (JMM Vertical Files, "Neighborhood: East Baltimore Research Packet: Carroll-Caton"); Dwight Warren interview, December 8 2005, OH 679, JMM; Francis X. Whittie, "Eastern Negro Area Devoid of Recreational Facilities," *Baltimore Sun*, May 13, 1945. The East Side Community Committee represented an African American district bounded by Baltimore Street on the south, Preston Street on the north, the Fallsway on the west, and Caroline Street on the east. Its southern portion included the northern part of Jonestown. The McKim Center, built by Quakers as the city's first free school in the 1820s, had long served as a charitable institution. According to current director Dwight Warren, segregation at the Center was the result of neighborhood custom, not McKim policy.

16   U.S. Census Bureau, U.S. Census of Housing, Maryland—Block Statistics, 1940 and 1950.

17   Ibid.

18   "Residents of Widened Fayette Street Worry about Unsightly Places," *Baltimore Evening Sun*, December 29, 1937.

19   Lucille Gorham interview, December 12, 1997, East Baltimore Oral History Collection, Langsdale Library Special Collections, University of Baltimore.

20   Rhonda Williams's study of public housing in Baltimore, *Politics of Public Housing*, offers an excellent analysis of the complex relationship between public housing officials and community advocates.

21   Clark S. Hobbs, "Those 275 Houses: What Can Be Done with Them?" *Baltimore Evening Sun*, January 20 1942. Blighted areas map is from HABC, *Twelve Questions: Annual Report, 1950.*

22   HABC Monthly Report, May 1950, 1.

23 Philip Darling, "HABC Considering Use of Elevator Buildings," HABC Quarterly Review, January 1952; "High Rise Housing: Does It Have a Place in the Public Housing Program?" *Journal of Housing* 9 (1952): 46; "Why the Argument?" *Journal of Housing* 9 (1952): 227-229.

24 "Dislocation and Relocation, Past and Future: Baltimore, Maryland," Baltimore Urban Redevelopment and Housing Agency (BURHA) Staff Monograph, 1965; Flag House Courts groundbreaking photo, *Baltimore Sun*, February 3, 1954. On desegregation of Baltimore's public housing, see Weiner, "From New Deal Promise to Postmodern Defeat," 210, and Williams, *Politics of Public Housing*, 106-113. BURHA was created in 1956 to oversee the city's housing authority and urban renewal agencies.

25 "Flag House Courts Project Launched by the Mayor," *Baltimore Evening Sun*, May 25, 1953; "Flag House Courts Site Similar to Ghost Town," *Baltimore Evening Sun*, May 29, 1953.

26 HABC, promotional brochure for Flag House Courts, circa 1955 ("Housing, Baltimore, Flag House Courts" Vertical File, African American Room, EPFL).

27 Ibid.; HABC press release, August 26, 1955.

28 Dudley P. Digges, "Altitude without Frills: A Glance at Apartments at Lafayette Courts," *Baltimore Evening Sun*, May 24, 1955.

29 HABC, A Report to the People of Baltimore!, 1953 Annual Report, printed in the *Baltimore Evening Sun*, May 25, 1954.

30 *Baltimore Sun*, November 19, 1955; U.S. Census Bureau, U.S. Census of Housing, Maryland—Block Statistics, 1960.

31 Esther Dortch interview, December 13, 2006, OH 702, JMM; Charles Dingle interview, January 17, OH 706, JMM. On the integration of Baltimore's housing projects, see Williams, *Politics of Public Housing*, 106-123.

32 Dingle interview; HABC, Y*our Investment: Annual Report, 1951*, 16; U.S. Census of Housing, Maryland—Block Statistics, 1970. On public housing and racial change, see for example Williams, *Politics of Public Housing*; Arnold Hirsch, *Making the Second Ghetto: Race and Housing in Chicago, 1940-1960* (New York: Cambridge University Press, 1983); Thomas J. Sugrue, *The Origins of the Urban Crisis: Race and Inequality in Postwar Detroit* (Princeton: Princeton University Press, 1996).

33 Williams, *Politics of Public Housing*, 96; Jackson, *Crabgrass Frontier*, 203-218.

34 Ann Faulkner Evans interview, January 10, 2007, OH 705, JMM; BURHA, "Types of Families Living in Baltimore's Low-Rent Projects, 1951-1964," unpublished report, 1965.

35 Evans, Dortch interviews; Scipio quoted in Michael A. Fletcher, "The Good Old Days at Flag House Courts," *Baltimore Sun*, November 18, 1993; Dorothy Scott interview, February 27, 2006, OH 680, JMM.

36 Scott interview.

37 Sheila Rosemond, cited in Michael A. Fletcher, "Residents Shed Tears, Share Memories," *Baltimore Sun*, February 11, 2001; Scott, Dortch, Evans interviews.

38 Lloyd B. Dennis, "Lombard Street Stores Offer Old World Variety," *Baltimore Sun*, August 12, 1964.

39 Scott, Dortch, Dingle, Evans interviews.

40 Julia Matthews interview, July 3, 2006, OH 693, JMM; Dortch interview. Almost all of the African Americans interviewed for this project were born in the South and came to Baltimore as children or young adults.

41 Thelma Lovelace interview, December 13, 2006, OH 701, JMM; Matthews, Dingle interviews.

42 Scott interview.

43 Lou Catalfo, quoted in Rafael Alvarez, "Pratt: The Dividing Line," *Baltimore Sun*, October 26, 1992.

44 Scott, Matthews, Lovelace, Evans, Dingle interviews.

45 Transportation projects started disrupting the neighborhood in the 1930s with the building of the Orleans Street Viaduct, which displaced Italian families who worked around Belair Market, and the widening of Fayette Street. These projects signaled a change in government priorities: increasingly, getting people in and out of the city in their cars took precedence over the quality of life for residents. Thomas W. Spalding and Kathryn M. Kuranda, *St. Vincent De Paul of Baltimore: The Story of a People and Their Home* (Baltimore: Maryland Historical Society, 1995), 116. On the industrial park, see Weiner, "From New Deal Promise to Postmodern Defeat," 215.

46 See for example Jackson, *Crabgrass Frontier*; Sugrue, *Origins of the Urban Crisis*; Williams, *Politics of Public Housing*.

47 *Baltimore Sun*, April 8 and 9, 1968; Dingle interview.

48 Dortch and Dingle interviews.

49 David Friedman, "Trouble Plagues Lombard Corned Beef Belt," *Baltimore Sun*, April 24, 1968; "Corned Beef Makes a Comeback," Baltimore Sun, May 6. 1968.

50 May 6 article above; various interviews.

51 Ralph Reppert, "Where Old World Flavors Linger: East Lombard Street Is an Island of Foreign Foods and Customs," *Baltimore Sun*, January 5, 1969.

52 Dingle interview; Reppert, "Where Old World Flavors Linger."

53 "Mayor Kicks Off Lombard Renewal," *Baltimore Sun*, April 3, 1976; Joyce Price, "Lombard Merchants' Beef: Road Repaving Hurts Sales," *Baltimore News-American*, October 11, 1976 (quote); Tracie Rozhon, "Fix-Up Stirs Lombard Street," *Baltimore Sun*, November 11, 1976.

54 *National Journal*, July 1, 1972; Baltimore City Department of Housing and Community Development (HCD), *Baltimore Public Housing, 1973 Annual Report*. HCD was the successor agency to BURHA.

55 Scott interview; HCD, Statistical Bulletin, second half, 1977; Baltimore City Department of Planning, "Jonestown Survey and Analysis," 1977: 4, 26.

56 Scott interview; Michael A. Fletcher, "No Way to Live," *Baltimore Sun*, May 9, 1993.

57 Dorothy Scott and Clara Butler, interview with author and Anita Kassof, Baltimore, January 9, 2006.

58 Exhibition files, Baltimore City Life Museums "Community Gallery" (Maryland Historical Society).

59 Edgar L. Jones, "Jonestown: A Section Only A Father Could Love," *Baltimore Sun*, November 12, 1976; Lawrence interview.

60 Quote is from Baltimore Heritage, Inc.'s report to the City Council on the proposal to create a Flag House Park, December 10, 1974 (located in files at CHAP).

61 Institutional archives, Jewish Museum of Maryland.

62 Gunts, "Plan for Community Wins National Award"; Tom Pelton, "New Life on Corned Beef Row," *Baltimore Sun*, June 3, 2001 (quote).

63 "Flag House Courts Project Overview," HABC, 2004; Scott and Butler interview.

64 Michael Anft, "Half Staff: Facing the End at Flag House Courts, the City's Last High-Rise Project," *City Paper*, December 22, 1999, and Anft, "Flag Down."

65 Dingle, Evans interviews.

141

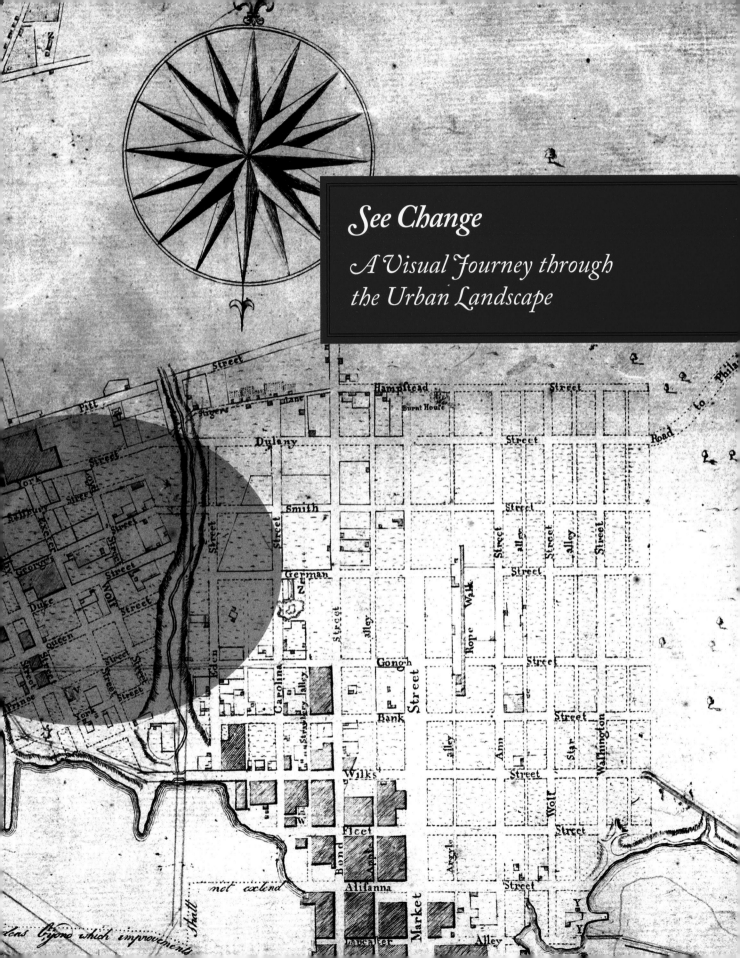

See Change

A Visual Journey through the Urban Landscape

For more than two centuries, image-makers have turned their gaze upon the section of East Baltimore portrayed in *Voices of Lombard Street*. The collective efforts of these mapmakers and painters, printmakers and photographers offer a compelling record of continuity and change in an urban landscape—and few places have changed as dramatically as this small neighborhood.

The images selected for this visual essay, therefore, serve as valuable historical evidence. By documenting the transformation of the built environment, they illuminate the historical processes that have shaped that environment. The following pages will show how open land on the edge of Colonial Baltimore turned into a convenient and desirable neighborhood for "genteel" Baltimoreans, then into a congested industrial age neighborhood inhabited by several waves of immigrants, and finally into two successive but vastly different federally subsidized experiments in urban renewal and social engineering.

Packed with information, these images reveal much about Baltimore's growth and development. But to truly grasp their significance, we must look at them as evocative springboards for asking deeper questions about the role of place in peoples' lives. To paraphrase Winston Churchill, humans shape their surroundings and, in turn, their surroundings shape them. These compelling images remind us how much place matters.

FROM THE FRINGES TO THE CENTER: EAST BALTIMORE, 1760S-1870S

For Sale or Rent—I will sell or rent my present dwelling, at the northwest corner of King George and Still House Streets [now Lombard and Front]. The house is spacious and convenient, with commodious 3 story back buildings, wash house, stable, etc. The situation is very healthy and pleasing, and not more than 200 yards from the Exchange and busy parts of the city, the neighborhood perfectly agreeable and respectable, and also convenient to 2 pumps of excellent water. J. Coulter

Baltimore American & Commercial Advertiser, March 22, 1822

The creation of Baltimore in 1729 on the north branch of the Patapsco River—above the city's present-day Inner Harbor—fueled decades of real estate speculation by investors hoping to cash in on the new town's future growth. Within three years, a rival town, Jones Town, emerged on ten acres east of the Jones Falls at Gay Street. But Baltimore Town's supremacy soon became obvious, and Jones Town merged with its larger neighbor in 1745. The neighborhood that arose in and around Jones Town's original boundaries became known as Oldtown.

In the late 1750s, merchant Jonathon Plowman, recently arrived from England, acquired 400 acres south and east of Oldtown, much of it along the Jones Falls. Plowman and another Englishman, Brian Philpot, began devel-

See Change: A Visual Journey through the Urban Landscape

BY DEAN KRIMMEL

Dean Krimmel is a public historian and museum consultant, and principal of Creative Museum Services.

OVERLEAF: *Detail of Folie's 1792 map of Baltimore, showing the earliest view of the Lombard Street neighborhood (highlighted).*

Courtesy of the Library of Congress Geography and Map Division.

oping the area by surveying land, laying out building lots, and naming streets. Their imprint is still apparent in the street grid pattern, remaining eighteenth-century homes, and English street names such as Albemarle, Exeter, and High.

Over the next fifty years, Baltimoreans filled much of the land along the waterfront, including Fells Point, a shipbuilding center blessed with deep water frontage. By the 1780s, the relatively undeveloped Oldtown area—located between downtown and Fells Point, the burgeoning city's two bustling ports—became a desirable residential locale. In the course of the next several decades, the neighborhood emerged as "*perfectly agreeable and respectable,*" conveniently tied to downtown wharves and counting houses by a series of bridges. Like other areas of the densely packed city (where walking was the primary means of transportation), it was home to a broad range of people, from wealthy property owners to the working poor, including whites, free blacks, and slaves. It boasted substantial winter "town homes" along with frame shanties, as well as numerous craft shops and small factories concentrated along the Jones Falls. The Phoenix Shot Tower, built in 1828, symbolized the growth of industry along the Falls.

Its architectural character established by 1840, the neighborhood saw its social landscape change fundamentally over the next two decades with the arrival of Irish and German immigrants, both Jewish and gentile. Meanwhile, more established residents began to move to newer and more fashionable neighborhoods. By the 1870s, the neighborhood bore little resemblance—socially and culturally, at least—to its former self. While remaining largely residential, it was now one of many second-hand districts where newcomers lived while working to improve their prospects.

The neighborhood east of the Jones Falls grew increasingly industrial throughout the nineteenth century. Here it is in the early twentieth century, with the Shot Tower (1828) predominating.

Courtesy of the Enoch Pratt Free Library, Central Library/State Resource Center.

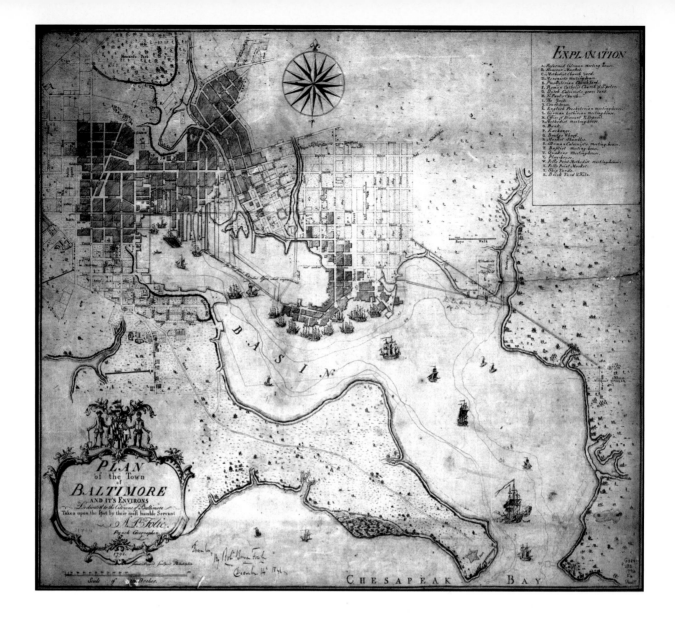

146

Between Town and Point

"Plan of the Town of Baltimore and its Environs,"
1792.

Engraving by A.P. Folie, courtesy of the Library of
Congress Geography and Map Division

Baltimore was America's biggest boomtown in the decades after the
Revolutionary War. And its fastest growing residential area lay east of the
Jones Falls and south of Fayette (then Wapping) Street. By 1792, property
owners—merchants such as Richard Caton and artisans such as candle-
maker Peter Boyd—were erecting houses and shops on streets that bore
names borrowed from Georgian London. Notice the shaded areas, indicating
improvements, and the dotted lines, representing future streets. Connected to
Baltimore's commercial center by bridges spanning the Jones Falls, the neighborhood was separated from the town's shipbuilding center at Fells Point by
another stream, Harford Run (now Central Avenue). Over the next fifty years,
builders would fill the empty spaces and knit together Baltimore's waterfront.

Along the Lower Falls

This painting by itinerant English landscape artist Francis Guy reveals the emerging neighborhood east of the Jones Falls. Appropriately, the view is dominated by the Falls and the Baltimore Street bridge, a vital link to the city center. Grouped near the bridge are the neighborhood's most substantial early buildings: the First Baptist Church, built in 1773 (at far left); a warehouse owned by merchant William Shields (with wharf); the imposing 1760 home of Brian Philpot, who owned much of the surrounding property (next to bridge); and the 1796 Christ P.E. Church (three chimneys). In the distance stands a row of four houses built by Charles Carroll of Carrollton in 1796. Beyond that is the Peters & Johnson brewery, built circa 1783. Guy's view captures the area's openness and demonstrates how city growth is the haphazard result of many individual acts—acquiring land, obtaining financing, building, and selling.

"View of the Presbyterian Church and all the Buildings as they Appear from the Meadow," 1804.

Oil on canvas by Francis Guy, courtesy of The Maryland Historical Society

An Urban Flavor, 1840s–1850s

View from the Shot Tower looking toward the east, circa 1850.

Daguerreotype by H.H Clarke, courtesy of The Maryland Historical Society

Decades of steady growth produced a dense neighborhood of two- and three-story brick rowhouses, as seen in this rare full-plate daguerreotype taken from the top of the Shot Tower at Fayette and Front streets. By the 1850s, the area was home to three synagogues: the Baltimore Hebrew Congregation's Lloyd Street Synagogue (1845), the Hebrew Friendship Congregation's Eden Street Synagogue (1848), and Har Sinai Verein (1849). The number of churches had grown to nine, from the old-line Friends Meeting House (1781) to churches built for recently arrived Irish and German immigrants, such as St. Vincent de Paul Roman Catholic Church (1840) and St. Matthew's Lutheran Church (1852). An aging native-born middle class of "gentlemen," merchants, lawyers, builders, sea captains, and small shopkeepers watched as young immigrants began finding work in local shops and factories—some renting homes from former residents.

A Jewish Presence in Classical Garb

Baltimore Hebrew Congregation dedicated its synagogue on Lloyd Street in 1845. The first built in Maryland, it remains the nation's third-oldest surviving synagogue. Designed by Robert Cary Long, Jr., a prolific local architect whose churches were widely admired, the Lloyd Street Synagogue was one of several early American synagogues rendered in the popular Greek Revival style. In Baltimore as elsewhere, the choice clearly indicated that congregants, upwardly mobile Jews of mostly German origin, intended to "fit in" and take their place within their city's middle class. Early congregants came from across the city, but the presence of a synagogue on Lloyd Street, as well as two others built nearby before 1850, drew Jewish newcomers to the neighborhood, setting the stage for its later transformation into "Jewish East Baltimore."

Lloyd Street Synagogue, circa 1864.

Carte-de-visite by D.R. Stiltz, Photographers, JMM 1997.71.1

150

Middle Class Gentility

Chesnut Home on East Baltimore Street, west of Aisquith Street, circa 1845.

Lithograph published by A. Hoen & Co., courtesy of The Maryland Historical Society

City life has always been a place of powerful contrasts and contradictions. In 1845, even as working-class immigrants began to make their presence felt, successful young Irish-born merchant William Chesnut built a genteel homestead on Baltimore Street—the type of residence more in keeping with newly developing areas on the outskirts of town. Located a block from the new synagogue on Lloyd Street, Chesnut's landscaped showplace was protected by a substantial iron fence, stylish cast iron gate, and generous set-back from the street. By the early 1880s, with its original occupants gone and the neighborhood's population again in transition, the old Chesnut home would be demolished.

A Quiet Slide from Respectability, 1850s–1870s

Within a single generation, the neighborhood lost most of its native-born middle class, whose former homes were rented by German, Irish, and native-born working-class families scrimping along on modest wages from skilled and unskilled jobs. The streets closest to the Jones Falls became decidedly more industrial, the old Peters & Johnson brewery being replaced by a large casket factory. Horsecar lines ran through the neighborhood, transporting the middle class from homes in fashionable new suburbs to downtown offices. As downtown grew in scale and importance, East Baltimore continued its quiet slide from respectability.

E. Sachse & Co.'s Bird's Eye View of Baltimore in 1869, detail.

Lithograph, courtesy of The Maryland Historical Society

SHTETL OR SLUM? JEWISH EAST BALTIMORE, 1880S-1940S

The old substantial houses . . . still remain. Formerly the residences of wealthy families, they were later on invaded by the foreign element of German and Irish nationality, but are now for the most part tenanted by a race from the East, the exiles and refugees from Russia.

Baltimore Sun, *August 24, 1895*

They crowd into tenement houses, eat unwholesome food, breathe impure air, shun water and despise soap. Their children are covered with several layers of dirt. Their women go unkempt, their men unwashed.

Jewish Exponent, *August 1887*

The arrival of thousands of Eastern European Jews, beginning in the 1870s and reaching a peak in the early 1900s, transformed the area east of the Jones Falls into an identifiable neighborhood: Jewish East Baltimore. The sheer quantity of newcomers who shared a religious and cultural background distinguished this era from the earlier period of Irish and German immigration. As members of these earlier immigrant groups advanced economically, they departed to suburban neighborhoods, helping to pave the way for the emergence of a new type of immigrant neighborhood: one which took on the characteristics of a classic ghetto.

Jewish East Baltimoreans came from small towns and cities in Lithuania, Poland, Latvia, Galicia, and Ukraine. They found work in downtown garment factories and in neighborhood sweatshops. They created a complex network of religious, educational, and social service institutions. Some opened businesses in rented storefronts, turning Lombard Street into the neighborhood's commercial center.

Despite its Jewish character, Jews shared the neighborhood with others during this era. Italians, who were busy constructing an ethnic neighborhood of their own across Pratt Street, and African Americans, mostly confined to alley streets, were the two largest non-Jewish groups.

Creating a Yiddish Market along Lombard Street, 1890s

Eastern European Jews transformed Lombard Street into an old world marketplace where modern city dwellers haggled over live chickens and geese, fruits and vegetables, meats, baked goods, and second-hand clothing. Much like Baltimore's public markets, including nearby Fells Point, Bel Air and Centre Markets, Lombard Street's Yiddish market helped immigrant shopkeepers gain an economic foothold and filled an important role as a public gathering place.

Woman and girls shopping on Lombard Street, circa 1880s.

Courtesy of the Ross J. Kelbaugh Collection, JMM 1988.226.3a

154

East Baltimore's Main Street

If Lombard Street was the colorful, public face of Jewish East Baltimore, then Baltimore Street was its cultural and intellectual center—especially the 1000-1200 blocks. A favorite parade route because of its generous width and easy access to downtown, East Baltimore Street boasted the neighborhood's most imposing buildings, as well as a jumbled assortment of social clubs, union halls, mutual aid societies, kosher restaurants, and Yiddish theaters.

Shown here from left to right are: the twin-spired Second Presbyterian Church, dedicated in 1852 on the site of the congregation's original 1805 church; Philanthropy Hall, home to the Baltimore Talmud Torah, the city's largest Hebrew school; a coffee and tea shop owned by Jewish immigrants Philip and Jennie Mirvis (the round sign advertises "Russian Teas"); and Carroll Hall, also known as the Labor Lyceum, a busy union hall offering office and meeting space to a variety of unions, from butchers and buttonhole stitchers to plasterers and pants makers.

Landsmanshaft *Shuls*

Eastern European Jews in America typically banded together with others
from their old country hometowns, forming mutual aid societies (*landsmanshaftn*) and synagogues (*landmanshaft* shuls). Lithuanian Jews from
the town of Pokroy became the first Eastern Europeans in Baltimore to
construct a synagogue. They formed Congregation Mikro Kodesh in 1886
and worshipped in a Pratt Street rowhouse before moving to their stylish
new Moorish Revival home on High Street in 1893. Baltimore's only onion-
domed synagogue, Mikro Kodesh remained active until 1942, long after most
Jewish congregations had left the neighborhood. When the congregation
dissolved, it sold the building to a machine shop operator, who occupied it
until the block was razed to make way for public housing in the 1950s.

*Looking north on the unit block of South High
Street, circa 1935.*

Photo by A. Aubrey Bodine, courtesy of the
Maryland Historical Society

Paid by the Piece

Six persons were probably fatally burned by the explosion of a gasoline stove and the fire which followed in a sweat-shop at 1424 East Pratt Street this evening.

Washington Post, May 9, 1895

Entrance to a sweatshop building.

Maryland Bureau of Industrial Statistics report, 1902, courtesy of the Maryland State Archives

Enterprising Eastern European Jews were acquiring property in East Baltimore by the 1890s. They subdivided rowhouses into smaller apartments, leasing space to clothing contractors, who converted them into sweatshops. The contractors, also Jewish immigrants, often lived in their sweatshops and worked alongside their employees. Sweatshop workers, predominantly Jewish but also Italian, Bohemian, Lithuanian, and African American, spent twelve to sixteen hours a day, six days a week, stitching collars, sewing hems and button holes, making pants and vests, fetching bundles, and pulling threads. Contractors often set impossible production quotas in response to pressure from larger factory owners, and then "sweated" the work out of their employees in cramped quarters that were not only breeding grounds for tuberculosis, but sometimes places of sudden danger.

An Entrepreneurial Spirit

East Baltimore proved fertile ground for those Eastern European Jews with the moxie, business acumen, and luck to become business owners. For most, it was a struggle that took years. Max Lapides (shown holding baby) came to Baltimore in 1897 with his pregnant wife, Mollie, and infant son, Joseph. By 1900, the thirty-five-year-old Polish Jew was working as a barber. Within a decade, Max had acquired a saloon at 819 East Pratt Street, where this photograph was taken. The family, now grown to six children, lived a few blocks away.

Max Lapides and family members in front of his East Pratt Street saloon, circa 1910.

Gift of Rose Sacks, JMM 1988.227.1

158

Lombard Street in the Auto Age

Looking east along the 1000 block of East Lombard Street, circa 1939.

Jewish East Baltimore reached its peak in the 1910s. By 1920, upwardly mobile Jewish families began to move out of the neighborhood, just as members of previous immigrant groups had done. But their departure, which accelerated over the next few decades, did not spell the end for businesses along Lombard Street. Joined by Italian grocery and produce sellers, Jewish shopkeepers continued spilling their wares onto the sidewalk for new customers and the many former residents who returned to shop—while erecting oversized, attention-grabbing signage demanded by the automobile age.

A Last Look

By the late 1940s, little remained of Jewish East Baltimore outside of Lombard Street and a handful of communal institutions. Corner service stations, light industrial buildings, and flop houses shared the streets with deteriorating rowhouses. The onion-domed Mikro Kodesh (seen in the middle of the image) housed a machine shop. The venerable Lloyd Street Synagogue would soon be abandoned and its neighbor, B'nai Israel, struggled to survive. Visible in the distance between the old neighborhood and Fells Point (at the upper left of the photo) is Perkins Homes, a World War II-era public housing project. As postwar city officials looked around for more sites to house the poor, they could not help but notice the badly aging former Jewish shtetl in East Baltimore.

View from the Shot Tower looking toward the southeast, 1949.

Photo by Jack Engeman, courtesy of The Maryland Historical Society

From Flag House Courts to Albemarle Square: Since the 1950s

By the late 1940s, the neighborhood was considered an exhausted relic of an earlier age, beyond redemption physically, economically, and socially. A prime candidate for "slum clearance" and "urban renewal," much of its land was acquired by Baltimore City and its buildings demolished to make way for public housing. In the 1950s, the construction of Flag House Courts, a nine-acre, $4.5 million, 487-unit development dominated by three twelve-story high rises, displaced 378 households and irrevocably altered the landscape.

Flag House Courts opened in 1955 as an integrated project but gradually its population became almost entirely African American. Like the Jewish immigrants of earlier days, black residents, many of whom had migrated from the rural South, entered their new neighborhood in great numbers and with few resources—and with significantly fewer opportunities. Through the 1960s, "working poor" families predominated, and the well-maintained projects afforded residents a sense of community. But life changed dramatically after the 1968 riots following the assassination of Dr. Martin Luther King, Jr. Local businesses closed, budget cuts crippled public housing maintenance, and the neighborhood became increasingly isolated. Conditions deteriorated over the next decades as residents coped with worsening poverty, joblessness, crime, and drug trafficking.

Meanwhile, civic-minded Baltimoreans had begun to rebel against the destruction of the city's architectural heritage inflicted by the process of urban renewal. Encouraged in the 1960s by a growing national preservation consciousness, historians and community groups began to rescue, refurbish, and open to the public the neighborhood's significant landmarks, including the Flag House, Carroll Mansion, Friends Meeting House, Shot Tower, McKim Free School, and Lloyd Street Synagogue (which grew into the Jewish Museum of Maryland). Activists also joined forces to address community needs. They formed the Jonestown Planning Council in 1974—giving the neighborhood a new name, Jonestown, based on its early origins. In its first decades, the Council established a day care center, successfully opposed the extension of the Jones Falls Expressway, won the placement of a metro stop, and helped create Shot Tower Park.

In the 1990s, city officials and community activists began to discuss demolishing Flag House Courts as part of a citywide plan to replace high-rise public housing. The 46-year-old complex was imploded in February 2001, making room for Albemarle Square, a mixed-income rowhouse development designed with extensive community input. This latest experiment in community planning and city living opens a new chapter in the life of East Baltimore. Local residents and community institutions also look to Jonestown's rich heritage—it was designated as a Baltimore City Historic District in 2003—as a tool to revitalize the neighborhood and a source of unending inspiration, fascination, and guidance.

Enter Public Housing

Flag House Courts, completed in 1955, reshaped the neighborhood. The public housing development was named for the nearby landmark that had been restored as an historic house museum in 1927 (a recent museum addition appears in center foreground).

Flag House Courts rises behind Baltimore's historic Flag House, March 1955

Photo by William Klender, courtesy of the Baltimore Sun Company, Inc., All Rights Reserved

The High-Rise Experiment

There is no better living-room view of the city anywhere.
Housing Authority of Baltimore City official, Baltimore *Sun*, August 29, 1955

Undated view of a Flag House Courts high rise.

Courtesy of Special Collections, University of Maryland Libraries

Planners of the 1950s embraced the modernist notion that high-rise apartments represented the best in city living—for rich as well as poor. High-density housing also stretched construction budgets, making high rises particularly attractive to public housing officials. Early Flag House residents later recalled the "good old days" before budget cuts in the 1970s and the influx of drugs changed the character of their neighborhood. By the 1980s, many people argued that such high rises had become warehouses for the poor—dehumanizing environments that bred crime, alienation, and poverty.

"Jewtown"

Everybody, I mean the whole neighborhood was down there. Everybody went to Jewtown to shop. Thelma Lovelace, East Baltimorean

Lombard Street continued to thrive in the 1950s and 1960s, attracting a diverse mix of customers. Flag House Courts residents and other black Baltimoreans shopped there in growing numbers, helping merchants cope with a dwindling of their traditional Jewish clientele. The street survived the 1968 riots relatively unscathed, though one business, Smelkinson's Dairy, burned down. (On nearby Gay Street, in contrast, rioters destroyed dozens of Jewish-owned stores.) Lombard Street bounced back, but the riots under-scored the changing nature of the neighborhood. Over the next couple of decades, many merchants decided it was time to close up shop or follow their white clientele to the suburbs.

View of the 1000 block of East Lombard Street, 1969.

Photo by A. Aubrey Bodine, copyright Jennifer B. Bodine, courtesy of www.aaubreybodine.com

164

A Shrinking Commercial Center

Corned Beef Row, 1986.

The official renaming of a section of Lombard Street as "Corned Beef Row" in 1976 helped the remaining delis bolster their tourist trade—locals never stopped coming—but it could not forestall the area's physical decline and departure of businesses. By the mid-1980s, the always-crowded Attman's Deli was surrounded by empty lots and a handful of bullet-proof carry out shops. Jack's Deli (now Lenny's) anchored Corned Beef Row to the east, its owners having enlarged and rebuilt their business as a cinder block fortress.

History Minded

Baltimore preservationists challenged the demolition-happy urban renewal mindset of the 1950s and 1960s by championing historically significant buildings that had fallen on hard times. Here, Women's Civic League members (left to right) Gina Patterson, Jane Zaharis, and Dolores Martin study architectural restoration plans for the former residence of Baltimore's second mayor, Thorowgood Smith. Built around 1794, 9 North Front Street is now a star attraction on the city's Heritage Walk, a pedestrian trail initiated by Jonestown cultural institutions to highlight the neighborhood's surprising number of surviving landmarks.

LEFT: *Restoration of 9 North Front Street, 1978.*

Courtesy of Special Collections, University of Maryland Libraries

RIGHT: *9 North Front Street, 2004.*

Photo by Carl Caruso, courtesy of Historic Jonestown, Inc.

Going, Going, Gone…

They pushed that button, you see it fall. Man, that was hurting. Seriously, I mean, that was my home. That was old Flag House. That was my stomping grounds.

Former Flag House Courts resident Charles Dingle

View of Flag House Courts demolition, February 2001.

Courtesy of Jamie and Vivian Makin, Phillyblast.com

On the morning of February 10, 2001, demolition experts used 200 pounds of dynamite to implode the three high-rise buildings of Flag House Courts, thus paving the way for neighborhood redevelopment.

The New Urbanism

Albemarle Square is a 15-square block urban community in the midst of an area rich in ethnic history . . . steps from world class shopping, dining, entertainment, sporting and cultural values.

From the website of Beazer Homes, co-developers of Albemarle Square, 2007

Planning for a post-Flag House Courts era began in 1998 with funding from the federal HOPE VI program, which encouraged the demolition of decrepit public housing and the creation of communities that blended with urban landscapes. Public sentiment, expressed in a series of design workshops, called for a mixed-use and mixed-income development with architecture similar to Baltimore's traditional rowhouse neighborhoods. A key feature was the restoration of the street grid system reconnecting residents to adjacent neighborhoods. The $47.5 million project, which won a design award from the American Institute of Architects, opened for occupancy in 2005.

Architectural Rendering of Albemarle Square.
Torti Gallas and Partners

A New Era

ABOVE: *View from the Shot Tower, 2007.*
Photo by Denny Lynch, JMM 2007.45.1

RIGHT: *Albemarle Square, 2007.*
Photo by Jennifer Vess

In these two images, Jonestown bears some striking similarities to the place it once was: a typical Baltimore rowhouse neighborhood. Albemarle Square reintroduced a human—and humane—scale, street-level residential density, and a diverse mix of people. Its residents enjoy convenience to work and shopping, access to cultural amenities, and historical charm. Reminders of the past are everywhere—from eighteenth-century street names and historic houses to the industrial age Shot Tower and Hendler Creamery building—and the neighborhood's cultural institutions are working hard to promote it as a heritage tourism destination. A new chapter in neighborhood life has begun and, with it, the search for a new identity.